MW01204938

Revealing THE END OF THE WORLD *to the* CHILDREN OF LIGHT

Rev. Brent Davis

WinePress Publishing
MUKILTEO, WA 98275

DEDICATION

To all Christians who seek the truth regardless of opposition and tradition, and to those for whom the Word of God is the final authority.

ACKNOWLEDGMENTS

To my wife and daughters who have encouraged me from the beginning; to the Grace of God in the lives of those who have financially supported this work; and to all those who have seasoned my life like salt.

CONTENTS

PROLOGUE

Can we know when Jesus will return to the earth? Can Jesus come at any unexpected moment? Will there be a "rapture" of the Church? Will we enter into tribulation? These are the questions that have driven me the past thirty years. I believe I have found the answers in the Word of God. Some have said, "He travels to the sound of a different drum." I believe, I am called of God. The message is true only if the calling is true. You be the judge.

I've had to change theologically in many areas pertaining to the prophecy of the return of Christ. I dare say, it was the most difficult undertaking I've gone through in life. I was entrenched in traditional doctrines and ideas. To break those bonds and to step outside the norm of thinking, left me on the outside with many of my colleagues. In this book, I've gone further than most ministers would dare. God has allowed me to break new ground. I know that the principles set forth in this book could well change pulpit messages across this land. There are still men that seek to hear the voice of God and do the will of the Lord, and they will remain true to correct doctrine.

In the Epistle of James, he writes, *"Wherefore, my beloved brethren, let every man be swift to hear, slow to speak, slow to wrath"* (James 1:19). What does it mean to hear the Lord? God spoke to Elijah and gave an illustration of how people perceive that God might speak to them:

> *And he said, Go forth, and stand upon the mount before the Lord. And, behold, the Lord passed by, and a great and strong wind rent the mountains, and brake in pieces the rocks before the Lord; but the Lord was not in the wind: and after the wind an earthquake; but the Lord was not in the earthquake:*
> *And after the earthquake a fire; but the Lord was not in the fire: and after the fire a still small voice.*
> *And it was so, when Elijah heard it that he wrapped his face in his mantle, and went out, and stood in the entering in of the cave. And, behold, there came a voice unto him, and said, What doest thou hear, Elijah?* (1 Kings 19:10-13).

If you have engrafted the Word of God in your heart, then God can and will speak to you. It's that still small voice that says, *"This is right and good—the thing to believe and do."* There are two things that keep us from hearing the Lord: weeds and ears that cannot hear. In the parable of the sower, Jesus spoke of the word that falls in a heart of thorns: *He also that received seed among the thorns is he that heareth the word; and the care of this world, and the deceitfulness of riches, choke the word, and he becometh unfruitful* (Matthew 13:22).

And into a heart that cannot hear:

When any one heareth the word of the kingdom, and understandeth it not, then cometh the wicked one, and catcheth away that which was sown in his heart. This is he which received seed by the way side (Matthew 13:19).

My prayer is that as you read this book, you can hear His voice.

CHAPTER 1

IT CAN HAPPEN!

Salvation

My first memory in life is a bar-ditch beside a country dirt road. I must have been three or four. I was playing with a toy bulldozer that was either battery operated or wind up. I remember that it was warm weather, so it wasn't Christmas or my birthday, which is also in the winter. The bottom of the ditch was full of sand deposited from the runoff after the rain, so that's why I was playing there. When Mother realized I was missing from the yard, she began to call my name and I crawled up out of the ditch to where I could be seen. Mom wasn't hysterical or anything because there were only a dozen families in all of Harpers Valley, so there wasn't much traffic. It is not the Harpers Valley of country music fame. We only had one community building and that was an old WPA, two-room schoolhouse that served only two teachers. We didn't need a PTA. The school grades were divided up into rows. Grades one through seven were in the first room and eight through twelve were in the second room. We lived directly across the road from this school because mom was the school cook. I started school at the age of five. I was there anyway, so why not.

This two room schoolhouse had an accordion-type divider that allowed the two rooms to be made into one large room, and every Sunday the residents of that rural community would meet there for church. They would push the desks to the outside walls, and then move the old oak pews to the center. There, they would worship God. Little did I know on the day of my first memory, I was just a few paces from what would become holy ground in my life.

Baptists have been having simultaneous revival meetings since Jesus and John the Baptist. So in the spring of 1953, we were having our meetings in that old schoolhouse. We called them meetings because a great deal of the time there was no revival happening. People had a lot less to repent of in those days. There was only one TV in the whole valley and at that time the state was voted non-alcoholic. Anyway, you have revival when God is ready for revival to happen. It is initiated by Him in response to the prayers of His people. I later came to realize that was exactly what happened, because folks, God showed up.

The evangelist for the meetings was Brother Jessie Jones and the song leader was Brother Don Queen. Both of these men had previously been pianists in bands that were on the other side of the fence, spiritually speaking. Even with prohibition in the state, there were still honky tonks and moonshine. We kids took to their playing, and would make our parents get there at least thirty minutes early to listen to them play and sing. The last I heard, they were still serving God.

It must have been during the last night of the meetings when I met God. I was five and my best friend, Dale Hall, was six. We were sitting on the fourth or fifth row. At the end of the sermon there was an invitation for anyone to come forward and make a public confession of their faith in Christ.

Whosoever therefore shall confess me before men, him will I confess also before my Father which is in heaven. But whosoever shall deny me before men, him will I also deny before my Father which is in heaven (Matthew 10:32-33).

Well, Dale leaned over and whispered, "I think I need to go down there. Will you go with me?"

"Sure," I said, and off we went down to the front. Dale was speaking to Brother Jessie and I was dangling my feet from the front pew without a thought in the world about what was happening. Brother Jessie and Dale knelt in prayer, and *doggone* if Dale wasn't born again at that very moment. He said it's true and I believe him. The next thing was really unexpected. Brother Jessie walked over to where I was sitting on the front pew and reached out and laid his hand on my shoulder. What happened was a miracle of God. I still go over it in my mind again and again, but it's always the same. It was just a miracle.

Brother Jessie was still speaking, but I was too engrossed in what I was seeing to answer a word. The whole north end of the church just vanished and I watched as a crowd of people climbed up to the top of a small hill. In the midst of the crowd, one person stood out because his robe was much whiter than all the rest. In fact, all the others seemed to be in a shadow. Their robes were all soiled and dark. Some of the men were carrying timber and some were soldiers. Then, at the age of five, I saw the Lord Jesus Christ nailed to one of those timbers. At that moment, I knew who Jesus was. God must have put it into my mind and heart, there is no other explanation. It must have been a few moments before I realized that Brother Jessie was asking me a question. I was busy watching God's theater in cinerama; but, and this is important, it was in black and white.

As I watched them going from my left to my right, Brother Jessie asked, "Do you know who Jesus is?"

"Yes, sir," I replied.

"Do you believe He died on a cross?"

"Yes, sir," I had just watched the whole thing and was wondering if everybody saw what I saw.

I had never seen a TV or movie at this time in my life. It wasn't something I could have dreamed up because there were no memories to relate to.

We had no indoor plumbing and barely had electricity. We drew water from a well and farmed with mules and a hand-held plow. We were so poor that poor people called us poor. Mother had a saying, "We might not have fine clothes, but we can be clean." She made sure that we were clean in both raiment and body.

Brother Jessie asked, "Are you sure?"

"Yes sir." I knelt and prayed for God to save me and for Jesus to enter into my heart. He did. When I stood up, I turned toward the north wall and the vision was gone. I hid it in my heart and never said anything to anyone about it. Dale and I were not baptized at that time. Our parents questioned whether or not we knew enough about what things were all about. They decided that if God moved us, then nothing could keep God from working His will into our lives. I still think this is pretty good advice, although I will never forbid any child from coming forward to confess Jesus Christ. I know it can happen. It happened to Dale— and to me, so it can happen to you.

Iowa Park

We left the valley about four years later. Dad worked in the federal service following World War II. Upon returning from a tour in the Navy, he discovered they had built a naval ammunition depot in McAlester, OK. Shortly after he began working there, they had a layoff and Dad transferred to Shepherd Air Force Base in Wichita Falls, TX.

Instead of trying to find a place in Wichita Falls, we located in a small town of about 13,000 called Iowa Park. Coming from a community that had only fifty kids in the whole school to one that had thirty in one class was tough. I remember the first day when I couldn't keep the tears from running down my face. I was determined to hang in there and I did. From this point until my senior year in high school, my life was just a normal kid's life. I only drank alcohol or smoked cigarettes in trial runs and decided they weren't for me. I had a wonderful childhood in a great town. I still love Iowa Park and the people who lived there. Some still live there. I never disliked any of the kids that attended school there and can honestly say they were more like brothers and sisters, in my way of thinking. I get melancholy, even now, when I think of them.

I played football, baseball and golf and managed to pass every year except one. In that one, I nearly died from complications with the mumps. Everyone thought I had contracted some terrible disease and were really disappointed to discover that it was only the mumps. Little do they know...

If you want to raise your kids in a great town, go to Iowa Park, Texas. I know it was God that sent me there. We had great teachers who cared for the students, and gave us an education that would take us as far as we wanted to go. They equipped us to face life.

The Call

In the spring of 1965, on Easter Sunday, my life was changed for the second time. My family had all gone to Faith Baptist Church. I didn't go. I told my mother I didn't think it was right for people to stay out of church all year, then get all dressed up on Easter just to show off their fancy clothes. So, I was staying home.

God makes house calls.

After a while of being alone in the house, I became bored. I thought I'd turn on the television set and see if there might accidentally be a baseball game on. This was 1965 and there were very few color television sets around. The national television companies were not so bold at that time, and usually wouldn't compete with church for the attention of the people. How things have changed.

I turned the set on and sat down on the divan. A moment later, I was on my face on the floor. There on TV, was a movie depicting the crucifixion of Christ. It was on an old black and white film—the exact one I had seen at the age of five in my vision. You can't convince me that God doesn't do miracles. I didn't need a sheepskin like in the story of Gideon— Judges 6:37—to tell me that this was God getting my attention. He had. That still small voice spoke, *"You're to preach the Gospel."*

Do you remember when I said that God responds to prayer? Well, I'm the youngest of four children. My three sisters are Annette, Betty and Sue. Dad was determined to have a son; so, when mom became pregnant with me, she wanted it to be the last time. She prayed to God and promised that if it was a boy, He could have her son to do His service. Well folks, God answers prayer and He came to collect.

I never explained the vision and the TV program to my parents. I simply told them that God had called me to be a preacher. I ask you, who would claim such a thing if it were not true? There are only a handful as successful as Billy Graham out there.

My parents encouraged me to speak with our pastor, Brother John Klappenbach. I walked forward the next Sunday and surrendered for the ministry. Brother John said, "The only way to know if God has called you to preach...is to preach." The following Sunday morning was to be the day. I was scared stiff, so I tried to keep it quiet at school, but the word got around.

That Sunday morning the church was full. Many of the students that I had grown up with were sitting in the congregation. I know they came to support me as their friend. I had been praying a lot that week that God would give evidence of His call on my life. I must have preached all of twenty minutes; but during the invitation there were several confessions of faith and some came to rededicate their lives to God. One of these was my father. I think there were seven in the group that came forward. Without a doubt, God showed His hand on my life.

The following spring I began my first semester at Oklahoma Baptist University. I was unprepared for the change from small town to large university, and failed to achieve a high enough grade point average to escape the draft. I discussed the matter with my father and decided to enlist in the Navy, instead of waiting to be drafted. My enlistment was for four years. The following year, my father was killed in an auto accident. Because of the backlog of troops being moved, I was three days catching a flight to the states. The Lord saw my family through that terrible time.

Vietnam

I'm a Vietnam veteran, as was my friend Dale Hall. We were saved together and we served together. I had the better part being in Naval aviation, while Dale slugged it out in the jungles and rice patties. The only thing any of us wanted was to come home alive. It didn't matter where I was, I knew the Lord had ordered my footsteps. I did two tours, starting in 1967 and finishing in 1970. No one who served there would ever be the same. If there was gold within, it was refined and made better. If a person had no foundation, they fell. And, great was their fall.

> *For other foundation can no man lay than that is laid, which is Jesus Christ. Now if any man build upon this foundation gold, silver, precious stones, wood, hay, stubble; Every man's work shall be made manifest: for the day shall declare it, because it shall be revealed by fire; and the fire shall try every man's work of what sort it is* (1 Corinthians 3:11-13).

Harpers Valley

After the death of my father, my mother moved back to Oklahoma. She had relatives that lived just a few miles from my place of Holy Ground. During the final three years of my military service, she remarried. Pat Jeffrey is a good man and I'm glad that he became a part of our family. When I was released, I came back to Oklahoma. I can remember landing at Oklahoma City and sitting down in the waiting area and then I passed out. In the combat zone, a person never really sleeps. It's a half-sleep, waiting for that sound that's out of the ordinary; and when you heard it, you came wide awake instantly. Having lived the last year in that type of situation, I finally slept. The next thing I remember was one of the rental car girls waking me and asking my name. It seems that my parents had been paging me for quite a while and I was oblivious to anything.

I lived and worked within five miles of the place of my salvation, but the war had taken its toll. I had lost the joy of that moment. His call on my life had become secondary to the fulfillment of those things which I had been denied over the last four years.

Five years passed. I married and became the father of two girls, Amy and Jamie. At the writing of this book, my wife, Patti, and I have been married for twenty-five years. I worked days and attended college at night, burning the candle at both ends trying to obtain material things. God had not forsaken me, and one day the call came.

Being confident of this very thing, that he which hath begun a good work in you will perform it until the day of Jesus Christ (Phillipians 1:6).

R. W. Sartor was a member of the Harpers Valley Baptist Church, and one day he called our home. The church was pastorless, and he had heard that I was licensed to preach. He wondered if I would come and bring a Bible study the next Sunday morning. I'm sure he knew that I hadn't preached in a long time, because he said they were not expecting too much. I wasn't expecting too much, either. I picked up my dusty Bible. I was sure God was in there somewhere. I read and studied and prayed, but there was no confidence within. That Sunday the Spirit came upon me and I preached the Gospel as though I had preached every day from the day that God had called me ten years before.

> *Then he answered and spake unto me, saying, This is the word of the Lord unto Zerubbabel, saying, Not by might, nor by power, but by my spirit, saith the Lord of hosts* (Zechariah 4:6).

This, then, is the point of this whole chapter: I became the pastor of the Harpers Valley Baptist Church. I had come full circle and no one could tell me that God had not done it. I was ordained a Southern Baptist minister at the very place where God saved my eternal soul. This is not an autobiography, it's a testimony of the wonderfulness of our Creator. Who else could write such a script? Who could think such a thought?

> *O the depth of the riches both of the wisdom and knowledge of God! how unsearchable are his judgments, and his ways past finding out!* (Romans 11:33).

22

CHAPTER 2

THE MESSAGE

I'm presently the pastor of Lehigh Baptist Church, Lehigh OK. Lehigh is the fifth church I've pastored in the past twenty years and the people are wonderful. We have a deep abiding love for one another. There is a freedom to preach that most pastors never find. I regret not having sufficient time to do all the things that are needful for the people that worship here.

It was during my second year that Travis Tollett, our Sunday school director, suffered a stroke. He was taken to the hospital in Oklahoma City in serious condition. I was on my way to be at his bedside, to do as much as possible in the way of comforting him. I was just outside of Shawnee, OK, when I was overcome by the Spirit of God. I pulled over to the shoulder of the highway and listened to the still small voice of the Lord.

We had been studying the book of Daniel and the prophecy of the final seven years leading up to the millennial kingdom of Jesus Christ. As I had been driving, I examined the Scripture in my mind, but there seemed to be something missing—something I wasn't seeing. I was silently praying when the light came on:

> *Ask, and it shall be given you; seek, and ye shall find; knock, and it shall be opened unto you* (Matthew 7:7).

God opened the Word and gave me the message you will find in the remainder of this book. It's not a story, it's a commentary on the Word. It may be difficult at times to accept and understand. If you ask the Spirit, he will give you the desire to seek; if you seek you will find the door upon which to knock; and if you knock, the door will be opened to you.

> *But the natural man receiveth not the things of the Spirit of God: for they are foolishness unto him: neither can he know them, because they are spiritually discerned.*
> *But he that is spiritual judgeth all things, yet he himself is judged of no man.*
> *For who hath known the mind of the Lord, that he may instruct him? But we have the mind of Christ* (1 Corinthians 2:14-16).

Therefore, the remaining chapters are about something that we can know: the future, The final seven years of history before the millennium and its event—the return of Christ.

Why is it Important?

Neglect not the gift that is in thee, which was given thee by prophecy, with the laying on of the hands of the presbytery.
Meditate upon these things; give thyself wholly to them; that thy profiting may appear to all.
Take heed unto thyself, and unto the doctrine; continue in them: for in doing this thou shalt both save thyself, and them that hear thee (1 Timothy 4:14-16).

It's important because God has given men the responsibility of making sure of their salvation; and not only theirs, but others that hear their doctrine.

We have also a more sure word of prophecy; whereunto ye do well that ye take heed, as unto a light that shineth in a dark place, until the day dawn, and the day star arise in your hearts (2 Peter 1:19).

Prophecy is made *more sure* by fulfillment in part. Fulfilled prophecy is a proof of inspiration because scriptural predictions of future events were uttered long before the events took place. Mere human foresight couldn't have anticipated them. These predictions are so detailed, minute and specific that they exclude the possibility of being fortunate guesses.

Hundreds of predictions—so ancient, singular, improbable and detailed that no mortal could have anticipated them—concerning Israel, the land of Canaan, Babylon, Assyria, Egypt, and numerous people have been fulfilled by natural elements, by men who were ignorant of them, those who disbelieved them or who struggled with frantic desperation to avoid their fulfillment. It is certain, therefore, that the Scriptures which contain them are inspired.

> *Prophecy came not at any time by the will of man; but holy men of God spoke as they were moved by the Holy Spirit* (2 Peter 1:21).

CHAPTER 3

EXPLAINING THE END
OF THE WORLD

The world will come to an end. The problem is under standing what we perceive that particular statement means. Just as the scriptural references infer that the world's beginning did not occur at the time of the creation of Adam, the end of the world is not synonymous with the return of Christ. Most refer to the return of Christ as the end of the world. Some consider the battle of Armageddon the end of the world. If these events are not the end of the world, then what is the end of the world?

In the book of Matthew, chapter twenty-four, there is a dialogue between the Apostles and the Lord Jesus. The apostles were in awe of the temple and the surrounding structures that were built during the reign of King Herod. Jesus remarked that, at some point in time, the stones of the present temple would be thrown down and not one stone would be left upon another. The natural response, from one of the apostles, came in the form of a three-part question. The first part of this three-part question was, *"Tell us, when shall these things be?"*

The following ten verses of Scripture (Matthew 24:5-14) covered the past 1,996 years. It could be argued that we are somewhere near verse twelve.

And because iniquity shall abound, the love of many shall wax cold (Matthew 24:12).

The Apostle Paul wrote in his second Epistle to the Thessalonians, that prior to the return of Christ there would come a falling away. His teaching is in harmony with the expression of the Lord that, *"And because iniquity shall abound, the love of many shall wax cold."*

Though there is revival in some countries, the majority of Christians have become complacent. The majority of church-goers are women and children. Our epitaph reads:

We began with twelve men
and we end with ten virgins.

The second part of the three-part question was, *"What shall be the sign of thy coming?"* This is where the confusion of those who fail to rightly divide the Scriptures occurs. The *sign* of the eminent return of the Lord Jesus Christ is something that can be known. It can be known because Christ explained it to the Apostles. It should destroy all other doctrines that teach the Lord returning without this particular sign. The belief that the Apostle Paul taught a secret "rapture" of the believers is contrary to biblical harmony.

The Abomination of Desolation

When ye therefore shall see the abomination of desolation, spoken of by Daniel the prophet, stand in the holy place, (whoso readeth, let him understand) (Matthew 24:15).

In Matthew 24:15, Christ refers to a portion of the Old Testament that indicates a future fulfillment of prophecy. From the time of Christ until the destruction of the temple in seventy A.D., there was no fulfillment of this prophecy. Though the Romans did destroy the temple, there is no historical record that they entered and placed an object to be worshipped. There is also no record that their general, Titus, proclaimed himself God from the portion of the temple called the Most Holy.

And the king shall do according to his will; and he shall exalt himself, and magnify himself above every god, and shall speak marvellous things against the God of gods, and shall prosper till the indignation be accomplished: for that that is determined shall be done (Daniel 11:36).

Let no man deceive you by any means: for that day shall not come, except there come a falling away first, and that man of sin be revealed, the son of perdition;

Who opposeth and exalteth himself above all that is called God, or that is worshipped; so that he as God sitteth in the temple of God, showing himself that he is God (2 Thessalonians 2:3-4).

The Apostle Paul, in his second Epistle to the Thessalonians, verified the prophetic text of the Lord and also verified that the event was yet future. He wrote of two signs that we can look for just prior to the appearing of Christ; the same two that Christ himself gave: A lack of love for God—a falling away—and the abomination of desolation spoken of by Daniel the prophet—the man of sin. Can we know when Christ is coming? Absolutely! Following the abomination of desolation, the man of sin will continue for three and one-half years, at a 360 day prophetic biblical year.

$$360 \times 3.5 = 1260 \text{ days}$$

And there was given unto him a mouth speaking great things and blasphemies; and power was given unto him to continue forty and two months (Revelation 13:5).

Forty-two months at thirty days a month, according to the Jewish lunar calendar which is New Moon to New Moon.

$$42 \times 30 = 1260 \text{ days}$$

And I will give power unto my two witnesses, and they shall prophesy a thousand two hundred and threescore days, clothed in sackcloth (Revelation 11:3).

1260 days would be three and one-half years, with years of 360 days.

The abomination of desolation is the second sign to precede His appearing.

Immediately following this event, there will be the Great Tribulation. Many who teach about the tribulation speak about a seven year period of time, but close examination of the prophecy of Daniel will reveal only a three and one-half year tribulation. It is this problem of scriptural doctrine on the subject of the return of our Lord, that the remainder of this book will attempt to reconcile.

The third part of the question was, *"And of the end of the world?"* Will the world come to an end? Yes, it will. The end of the world is not to be confused with the return of Christ. Christ's answer to the third part of the question, is not to be applied or confused with the second part of the question, bearing on His return to establish His kingdom over a reunited Israel.

Heaven and earth shall pass away, but my words shall not pass away.
But of that day and hour knoweth no man, no, not the angels of heaven, but my Father only (Matthew 24:35-36).

Many read this scripture and will say," See, no one can know when Christ will return." The true response is, that no one can know when the world will come to an end, but we can know when Christ will establish His kingdom. The end of the world will not come for at least one thousand years after the return of the Lord to establish His kingdom upon the earth. Following the one thousand years, there will be the beginning of the eighth, or eternal, day. Even at this point, it is uncertain whether or not the world is destroyed. It could be much later that the world will be dissolved.

CHAPTER 4

THE FINAL SEVEN

I doubt that there was a more controversial subject in the New Testament Church than that of the last seven years of the prophecy of Daniel's seventy sevens. Most Bible students agree that the last seven years is still yet future, but fail to agree on almost every aspect of that period of time. This is not only across denominational lines, but interdenominational, as well. In any congregation, you will find: pre-, mid-, and post-tribulation believers.

Pre-tribulation doctrine is the belief that the return of Christ for the Church will occur at the beginning of the last seven years His return to rule and reign for a millennium will come at the end of the seven years.

Mid-tribulation doctrine differs only in that the return of Christ for the Church will take place midway through the last seven years, then following three and one-half years of tribulation, Christ will return to establish His kingdom.

Post-tribulation doctrine is the belief that Christ will only return at the end of the seven years to establish His kingdom, and that the Church will not be taken prior to that time.

It is difficult to understand how there can be so many different interpretations when we all have the same Scripture to base our opinions upon. We can't all be right!

I do not think it is a question of being evil, only in error.

Error

> *Jesus answered and said unto them, Ye do err, not knowing the Scriptures, nor the power of God* (Matthew 22:29).

This particular passage of Scripture is referring to the Saducees, who did not believe in the resurrection of the dead. The answer Jesus gave them was so simple.

> *And as touching the dead, that they rise: have ye not read in the book of Moses, how in the bush God spake unto him, saying, I am the God of Abraham, and the God of Isaac, and the God of Jacob?*
> *He is not the God of the dead, but the God of the living: ye therefore do greatly err* (Mark 12:26-27).

The answer to the doctrinal questions or the disputes concerning the events of the last seven years could be just an error in knowing the Scriptures. The answer lies in the Scripture and we must endeavor to find it.

34

All Scripture is given by inspiration of God, and is profitable for doctrine, for reproof, for correction, for instruction in righteousness (2 Tim 3:16).

These men were a part of the ruling religious leaders of the nation of Israel, how could they interpret the Scripture incorrectly? Sounds familiar.

There was a preacher, by the name of Apollos, whose ministry started about the time Christ died.

And a certain Jew named Apollos, born at Alexandria, an eloquent man, and mighty in the Scriptures, came to Ephesus.

This man was instructed in the way of the Lord; and being fervent in the spirit, he spake and taught diligently the things of the Lord, knowing only the baptism of John.

And he began to speak boldly in the synagogue: whom when Aquila and Priscilla had heard, they took him unto them, and expounded unto him the way of God more perfectly (Acts 18:24-26).

It seems apparent that Apollos was a student of the teaching of John the Baptist. He probably proclaimed the Gospel something like, "Make straight your paths because the Messiah is coming to establish His kingdom on the earth." In verse twenty-five, the Scriptures allude to this by referring to the baptism of John. Why did John baptize?

And I knew him not: but that he should be made manifest to Israel, therefore am I come baptizing with water (John 1:31).

John was sent to prepare the way of the Messiah who would fulfill the promise of a kingdom for the nation of Israel. His baptism was one of repentance for those who believed his message that the kingdom was at hand.

Apollos continued to proclaim the earthly kingdom, until he received instructions from those who were closer to, or those that were more familiar with, the continuing revelation for the establishment of the Church.

Was Apollos evil? Of course not!

Was Apollos in error? I think there are many preachers in the same situation as Apollos, unmindful of the continuing unveiling of the mysteries of the kingdom of God. The truth is, he had not received the full revelation of the ministry of the gospel of grace. The Scriptures themselves say that there are some revelations that are sealed until the time of the end. Error occurs when we fail to establish a connection of Scripture with the proper dispensation.

I sometimes wonder how Apollos took additional instruction from Aquila and Priscilla. If I went to some of my brothers and sisters in Christ, expounding unto them a continuing revelation beyond what they have already been taught, how would they react?

According to Scripture, Apollos continued in the ministry, accepting the fuller revelation. Then, in Paul's first letter to the Corinthians (1:12; 3:4-6, 22; 4:6) Apollos was equated status equal to that of himself or Peter.

There are scriptures that indicate a full revelation will occur as we near the end of the age. Will this revelation be given to every Christian individually, or, as in the case of Apollos, will it be given to some to share with the rest of the Church?

But thou, O Daniel, shut up the words, and seal the book, even to the time of the end (Daniel 12:4).

I believe we are nearing the end and could actually be in the last seven years leading up to the establishment of the kingdom of our Lord without being aware of it. There are three things concerning the final seven years that I believe everyone can agree on. These three are: a beginning, middle, an end, and the events that correspond to these periods.

As we near the end of the age, God is beginning to break the seals that have bound the meanings of the Scriptures. We will see, in the near future, the unveiling of prophecies as no other generation.

The Beginning

The final seven years will begin with a confirmation of a covenant concerning the nation of Israel. It will be with an individual or a group that will be supported by the Man of Sin, or Antichrist.

The Middle

The next item is the desecration of the temple and the cessation of offering animal sacrifices at the middle of the seven years. Daniel prophesied that there would be a return to the sacrificial system and during the last seven years the man of sin would commit the abomination of desolation.

And in the midst of the week he shall cause the sacrifice and the oblation to cease, and for the overspreading of abominations he shall make it desolate (Daniel 9:27).

37

At what point in time the animal sacrifices will begin again is anybody's guess. It could be that they will begin during the seven final years, a part of the agreement that is supported by the Antichrist. One thing is sure. This person will not allow any worship that does not center around himself. For this very reason, the sacrifices could not take place for any length of time.

> *Who opposeth and exalteth himself above all that is called God, or that is worshipped; so that he as God sitteth in the temple of God, showing himself that he is God* (2 Thessalonians 2:4).

Satan's desire has always been to be exalted above God. His rebellion caused the fall of one-third of the angels and his expulsion from heaven. As prince of this world, he now attempts to rule through man.

> *For thou hast said in thine heart, I will ascend into heaven, I will exalt my throne above the stars of God: I will sit also upon the mount of the congregation, in the sides of the north* (Isaiah 14:13).

> *And he said unto them, I beheld Satan as lightning fall from heaven* (Luke 10:18).

> *And his tail drew the third part of the stars of heaven, and did cast them to the earth* (Revelation 12:4).

The man of sin will accept the offer of a worldly rule that Jesus refused during His temptation in the wilderness.

Satan has no power on the earth, unless he uses an earthly body—either animal or human. We are charged in Scripture not to give place to the devil.

Neither give place to the devil (Ephesians 4:27).

The term *give place* seems to indicate moving aside or allowing entrance. Demons are disembodied spirits seeking habitation, that they might manifest themselves in physical actions on behalf of Satan. Satan entered only one person and that was Judas Iscarot.

And after the sop Satan entered into him. Then said Jesus unto him, That thou doest, do quickly (John 13:27).

Satan did not enter into the serpent as some suppose, at least the Scriptures do not state that this was the case. In fact, the Scriptures do not say that the serpent was an animal. We come to that conclusion based on the curse that was placed on the serpent. It could be that the serpent was actually Satan.

Now the serpent was more subtle than any beast of the field which the Lord God had made (Genesis 3:1).

And the Lord God said unto the serpent, Because thou hast done this, thou art cursed above all cattle, and above every beast of the field; upon thy belly shalt thou go, and dust shalt thou eat all the days of thy life (Genesis 3:14).
And the great dragon was cast out, that old serpent, called the Devil, and Satan, which deceiveth the whole world (Revelation 12:9).

Demons, on the other hand, do enter men and animals (Matthew 5:2-15). It is unclear where these spirits come from. The Scriptures indicate a distinction between fallen angels and *devils*, translated from the Greek, *daimonion*.

For if God spared not the angels that sinned, but cast them down to hell, and delivered them into chains of darkness, to be reserved unto judgment (2 Peter 2:4).

And the angels which kept not their first estate, but left their own habitation, he hath reserved in everlasting chains under darkness unto the judgment of the great day (Jude 1:6).

So, it seems that demons are allowed to roam the earth at will, while the fallen angels are kept until Judgment Day.

The man of sin might possibly be under the control of some demon, but the Scriptures do not indicate that Satan will dwell in, or possess, his physical body. The Scriptures indicate a willingness to worship Satan; to do his bidding in return for the promises of worldly wealth, prestige and worship by humans.

The abomination of desolation will be a desecration of the temple by the man of sin. He will enter the Most Holy Place, a place the High Priest enters only once a year, and proclaim himself God. He will place an object or statue on, or in, the temple. When this occurs, the Jewish people will understand that the man they thought was the Messiah was actually an advocate for Satan. They will begin to flee as they did in Germany under the persecution by Hitler. Jesus issued a warning for those in that generation:

When ye therefore shall see the abomination of desolation, spoken of by Daniel the prophet, stand in the holy place, (whoso readeth, let him understand) (Matthew 24:15).

Then let them which be in Judaea flee into the mountains (Matthew 24:16).

This object, or statue, will have tremendous powers that Satan will bestow upon it:

And he had power to give life unto the image of the beast, that the image of the beast should both speak, and cause that as many as would not worship the image of the beast should be killed (Revelation 13:15).

There is a great similarity to these events found in the book of Daniel. Nebuchadnezzar, the king of Babylon, had a golden statue constructed in his likeness and everyone was instructed to kneel before the statue whenever musical instruments were played. If you didn't bow down to worship the statue, you were to be put to death.

Daniel places the abomination of desolation at the midpoint of the last seven years:

And he shall confirm the covenant with many for one week: and in the midst of the week he shall cause the sacrifice and the oblation to cease (Daniel 9:27).

Consider that the last seven years are a total of 2,520 days, with the biblical prophetic year of 360 days. Then, the middle would be 1,260 days, or as in the book of the Revelation, forty-two months:

And there was given unto him a mouth speaking great things and blasphemies; and power was given unto him to continue forty and two months (Revelation 13:5).

These forty-two months are the last half of the seven year period. The Antichrist only receives power from Satan at the midpoint and begins his reign of terror which lasts three and one-half years.

There are two events that will coincide with the Antichrist being revealed. As we have mentioned before, the people of Israel will flee from the city; and according to the teachings of Christ, following this occurrence there will be the Great Tribulation.

For then shall be great tribulation, such as was not since the beginning of the world to this time, no, nor ever shall be (Matthew 24:21).

The question is, was there a tribulation before this Great Tribulation? The scripture previous to this particular verse says there would be: war, racial war, famine, pestilence, earthquakes, deceptions, iniquities, loss of brotherly love; and that Christians would be afflicted, betrayed and hated. Sounds like the times in which we are now living. If you consider these things as tribulation, then, there will be tribulation the whole seven years. If you do not consider these things as tribulation, then only after the abomination of desolation will there be tribulation.

Will we know if we have entered into the last seven years before the desecration takes place? Satan knows that he can not dump the whole evil plan of world domination at one time. The human race is slowly being consumed by the wiles of the devil. We are gradually being programmed to accept the rule of the Antichrist. We are slowly being brought into bondage to the world system, becoming more and more dependent upon the governments of the world for our living.

The Antichrist

During the last three and one-half years, the Antichrist will attempt to control the whole world and every person on the earth. His attempt will be both spiritual and economical. He will attempt to destroy those who worship Christ.

I beheld, and the same horn made war with the saints, and prevailed against them (Daniel 7:21).

And it was given unto him to make war with the saints, and to overcome them: and power was given him over all kindreds, and tongues, and nations (Revelation 13:7).

Just a word about saints. The word *saint,* in Scripture, refers to those who have been redeemed from among mankind. All believers are saints:

Unto the church of God which is at Corinth, to them that are sanctified in Christ Jesus, called to be saints, with all that in every place call upon the name of Jesus Christ our Lord, both theirs and ours (1 Corinthians 1:2).

As the Antichrist attempts to destroy the Christians, he will attempt to mark every living soul:

> *And he causeth all, both small and great, rich and poor, free and bond, to receive a mark in their right hand, or in their foreheads* (Revelation 13:16).

The word *mark* used in this passage of Scripture is defined as a scratch or etching. The process now being developed calls for the implantation of a microchip in the hollow of the right hand or on the forehead. This mark, number or name, will be the only means to buy or sell; and many will sell their soul for a crust of bread:

> *And that no man might buy or sell, save he that had the mark, or the name of the beast, or the number of his name* (Revelation 13:17).

> *To have respect of persons is not good: for for a piece of bread that man will transgress* (Proverbs 28:21).

> *And I saw one of his heads as it were wounded to death; and his deadly wound was healed: and all the world wondered after the beast* (Revelation 13:3).

Those who have wealth and worldly goods in that day will find it hard to resist taking the mark of the beast. If you can imagine: no electricity without the mark, no water. You can't pay the bills without the mark. No social security or retirement check in the mail. There will be no employment without the mark, and no health care. All the wealth and worldly goods will be gone without the mark. That is why Jesus said, "*And again I say unto you, It is easier for a camel to go through the eye of a needle, than for a rich man to enter into the kingdom of God*" (Matt. 19:24).

The Days of Lot

I like to draw a parallel to the scripture in which Jesus is speaking to the disciples about the end, trying to give them an idea of what it will be like.

Likewise also as it was in the days of Lot; they did eat, they drank, they bought, they sold, they planted, they builded; But the same day that Lot went out of Sodom it rained fire and brimstone from heaven, and destroyed them all. Even thus shall it be in the day when the Son of man is revealed (Luke 17:28-30).

One thing about the days of Lot that is not mentioned here is the story of Lot's wife turning into a pillar of salt. Lot was commanded to leave the city without any of his possessions. The desire of the things left behind caused his wife to be disobedient and look back. There will be many like Lot's wife. The things of the world will have such a strong power over them that they will forfeit their soul for the desire of worldly goods.

The reign of the Antichrist will start at the middle of the seven years and will be manifest by the mark of the beast. The Scriptures teach that this abomination will be the revealing of the Antichrist.

CHAPTER 5

THE END

The end of the seven years is known as the battle of Armageddon. This word is found only once in Scripture, but is known by all the world. It is man's description for the end of the world, yet it is not the end of the world. The battle of Armageddon and the return of Christ are synonymous. They occur at the same time. During the last three and one-half years, there will be many battles, and this will be the culmination of all those battles. The Bible calls this the *Day of the Lord*.

Any day has a beginning. When morning comes, we call it a new day while there are hours yet to go. This is the same as the Day of the Lord.

The Day of the Lord is going to be a thousand years. This battle and the return of the Lord are just the beginning of that day.

> *But, beloved, be not ignorant of this one thing, that one day is with the Lord as a thousand years, and a thousand years as one day* (2 Peter 3:8).

There is other biblical evidence that a thousand years is considered a day with the Lord. Consider the declaration of God when speaking to Adam concerning the eating of the forbidden fruit and the penalty that it will incur:

> *But of the tree of the knowledge of good and evil, thou shalt not eat of it: for in the day that thou eatest thereof thou shalt surely die* (Genesis 2:17).

We know from biblical history, that Adam lived to be 930 years old. But, he didn't live to be one thousand; and, thus, being a fulfillment of what Peter wrote through the inspiration of the Holy Spirit. It also confirmed the scripture that God can not lie:

> *God is not a man, that he should lie; neither the son of man, that he should repent: hath he said, and shall he not do it? or hath he spoken, and shall he not make it good?* (Numbers 23:19).

Adam died in his and God's day.

There is yet another confirmation in Scripture which will be dealt with in greater detail in a later chapter on the *resurrections*—found in the Gospel of John seven times:

> *Martha saith unto him, I know that he shall rise again in the resurrection at the last day* (John 11:24).

The phrase *at the last day*, could designate that the resurrection will take place at the beginning of a particular millennium.

Armageddon

In the Revelation of Jesus Christ, John was given a scroll and told to eat it. The angel said it would be sweet in the Apostle's mouth, but bitter in his stomach. The Day of the Lord will be that way. We all earnestly look for the return of the Lord and that promise is sweet to the taste. But the kingdom in which we will rule and reign with Christ, will only be established after Armageddon and the destruction of all evil on Earth.

And he gathered them together into a place called in the Hebrew tongue Armageddon (Revelation 16:16).

The forces that gather will battle each other to determine who will rule over the world. There will be armies from the north, east, and south. As these armies gather to fight each other, the true ruler of the universe will return to claim His throne. His name is Jesus Christ. There is actually no conflict between Christ, His saints and the earthly forces. The battle is won by the word of the Lord:

And out of his mouth goeth a sharp sword, that with it he should smite the nations (Revelation 19:15).

And the remnant were slain with the sword of him that sat upon the horse, which sword proceeded out of his mouth (Revelation 19:21).

And the sword of the Spirit, which is the word of God (Ephesians. 6:17).

All who are in the valley will be destroyed. Only those who did not go to war will survive. This will bring about the fulfillment of the Sermon on the Mount:

Blessed are the meek: for they shall inherit the earth (Matthew 5:5).

After the battle of Armageddon, Christ will establish His kingdom over the remaining people of the earth; those who were meek and unwilling to be a part of the armies gathered to do battle in the valley north of the city of Jerusalem. I do not understand how the weapon of the Word of the Lord slays the armies. The Scriptures say that the valley will be full of blood. I do know that life is in the blood, maybe their blood must be shed.

For the life of the flesh is in the blood (Leviticus 17:11).

And the winepress was trodden without the city, and blood came out of the winepress, even unto the horse bridles, by the space of a thousand and six hundred furlongs (Revelation 14:20).

The valley of Jezreel, sometimes called Meggido, will be the encampment of the forces of the Antichrist. From this position, he will attempt to subdue all of the countries of the world and defeat the armies that gather to battle for the control of Jerusalem. I can not say why all the nations will want to control Jerusalem, but the Scriptures confirm this to be true:

> *But tidings out of the east and out of the north shall trouble him: therefore he shall go forth with great fury to destroy, and utterly to take away many. And he shall plant the tabernacles of His palace between the seas in the glorious holy mountain; yet he shall come to His end, and none shall help him* (Daniel 11:44-45).

> *And in that day will I make Jerusalem a burdensome stone for all people: all that burden themselves with it shall be cut in pieces, though all the people of the earth be gathered together against it* (Zechariah 12:3).

Though the world's system will have great power, it will not control all people. If it were true, where do the armies come from? Those that will be controlled will be those that choose to become a part of the system by receiving the mark, number or name of the beast. They forfeit their souls for the pleasures and material gain of this world. There will be many who do not receive the mark of the beast because they reject the Antichrist. Studying the Scriptures, we can see a group of people who do not accept Christ or the Antichrist. It is over this group of people that Christ will establish His kingdom. The majority of survivors will be the remnant of the nation of Israel.

> *And it shall come to pass, that every one that is left of all the nations which came against Jerusalem shall even go up from year to year to worship the King, the Lord of*

hosts, and to keep the feast of tabernacles (Zechariah 14:16).

And I will bring the third part through the fire, and will refine them as silver is refined, and will try them as gold is tried: they shall call on my name, and I will hear them: I will say, It is my people: and they shall say, The Lord is my God (Zechariah 13:9).

I will cover the Day of the Lord; the resurrection and translation of the saints; and the reign of Christ over the inhabitants of the earth, in subsequent chapters.

Most students of the Bible agree on the three events I have written of in this chapter: the beginning, a covenant of seven years; the middle, the abomination of desolation; and the end, the battle of Armageddon.

CHAPTER 6

WHO WILL BE TAKEN?

P re-tribulation doctrine teaches that the Church of our Lord will be translated—raptured—into the spiritual realm prior to the beginning of the last seven years of some particular millennium. Most of this teaching revolves around three or four scriptures that I will bring into view in this chapter for closer evaluation. I've read other writers' interpretations, so, I will add mine to the list. Dare to read another view point.

The Days of Noah

> *But as the days of Noe were, so shall also the coming of the Son of man be* (Matthew 24:37).

In the days of Noah, there were several things occurring at or about the same time. We should look around us and try to identify any of those events happening today.

The days of Noah could be interpreted as the two thousand years before the flood, not the 950 years that he actually lived:

> *And all the days of Noah were nine hundred and fifty years: and he died* (Genesis 9:29).

Take into consideration the prophetic scripture from the Apostle Peter, *"One day is with the Lord as a thousand years."* *Days*, plural, could mean two or more. Consider that we are nearing the two-thousand-year mark from the birth of Christ. The Scriptures record two thousand years under Adam (the days of Noah), two thousand years under Moses (the law,) and two thousand years under Christ. Is the history of creation laid out in a week, with days as thousands of years? If it is, then the last day would only be one thousand years.

$$(2 + 2 + 2) = 6 + 1 = 7$$

> *Blessed and holy is he that hath part in the first resurrection: on such the second death hath no power, but they shall be priests of God and of Christ, and shall reign with him a thousand years* (Revelation 20:6).

We can see a similarity in the two-thousand year time frame, two bi-millennial dispensations: two days before the flood, 2000 years; and two days before the destruction of the earth with fire, 2000 years.

Prior to the flood, the Scriptures speak of the attempt to destroy the purity of the human race by fallen angels.

Genetic Intervention

> *That the sons of God saw the daughters of men that they were fair; and they took them wives of all which they chose* (Genesis 6:2).

The term *sons of God* is used in Scripture to refer to angels five times—Old Testament (Job 1:6, 2:1, 37:8, Genesis 6:2,4)—and to the redeemed, six times—New Testament (John 1:2, Rom. 8:14,19, Phil. 2:15, 1 John 3:1,2). Could it be that we are replacing the fallen angels in the kingdom of God? The attempt to destroy the seed of Eve would mean that the redeemer could not come from man, and the prophecy would be broken.

> *And I will put enmity between thee and the woman, and between thy seed and her seed; it shall bruise thy head, and thou shalt bruise his heel* (Genesis 3:15).

Christ, the seed of Eve, had his heel bruised on the cross of Calvary. Satan's head was bruised by the blood of the Lamb of God shed for our remission of sin.

> *And you, being dead in your sins and the uncircumcision of your flesh, hath he quickened together with him, having forgiven you all trespasses;*
> *Blotting out the handwriting of ordinances that was against us, which was contrary to us, and took it out of the way, nailing it to his cross;*

> *And having spoiled principalities and powers, he made a show of them openly, triumphing over them in it* (Colossians 2:13-15).

If Satan attempted to introduce genetic manipulation before the time of Noah, then at the end he will attempt to do the same. Genetic manipulation sounds like our day and time. Soon, we will see the results of test tube babies and artificially inseminated births. The Antichrist will indeed be born of a virgin. How else could he claim the throne? How else could the people of Israel accept him as the Messiah?

The Scriptures speaking of Noah, say that he was perfect in his generations:

> *These are the generations of Noah: Noah was a just man and perfect in his generations, and Noah walked with God* (Genesis 6:9).

Does this mean that the descendants of Noah had not been altered by genetic manipulation? It also sheds light on the particular epitaph that God brings against the people of that day:

> *For as in the days that were before the flood they were eating and drinking, marrying and giving in marriage, until the day that Noe entered into the ark* (Matthew 24:38).

They were *eating* and *drinking*. This particular scripture is not describing excess in this instance. Gluttony is a sin, as is over indulgence in alcoholic beverages. Heaven knows that there is such in the world today. But, there is a far greater problem arising in our generation and that is the genetic manipulation of the foods we eat. There has been an alteration of at least two substances that are in our diet today: milk and tomatoes.

Cattle are being genetically engineered to produce more milk that has a longer shelf life; and tomatoes have been genetically engineered not to rot, having an indefinite shelf life. What will these products do to the human body? Are we a product of what we eat? They were eating and drinking in the days of Noah. What were they eating and drinking? The term *eating and drinking* is found ten times in the Word of God; six times in the Old Testament and four times in the New Testament. There is a different wording in the Greek language used for this particular passage of Scripture. I believe that difference indicates that it does not have gluttony in view.

The most important and most often overlooked scriptural reference about how it was in the days of Noah follows:

> *And knew not until the flood came, and took them all away; so shall also the coming of the Son of man be* (Matthew 24:39).

The ones taken away, according to this scripture, are the ones who did not believe.

Noah preached for 120 years that judgment was coming upon the earth, yet he did not gain one convert. Then, the flood came and destroyed the unbelievers off the face of the earth. Therefore, the succeeding verses depict taking away the ungodly of the earth, and not the expected and unscriptural *rapture* of the Church:

> *Then shall two be in the field; the one shall be taken,*
> *and the other left.*
> *Two women shall be grinding at the mill; the one shall*
> *be taken, and the other left* (Matthew 24:40-41).

The ones taken away, here, are not believers that meet the Lord in the air. Taken in context, they are the ones that will be taken away in death during the tribulation.

It has been the practice of God, in past history, to visit judgment upon the ungodly, taking them away in destruction of the physical body. In the future, it will be no different. There is a judgment found in Matthew twenty-five, that takes place after the tribulation, and prior to the establishment of the kingdom of our Lord. The order of events will be: the resurrection of the dead in Christ, the translation of those believers who live through the tribulation, and the gathering of the remnant of Israel with the Gentiles that are left that did not worship the Antichrist. Specifically, those Gentiles who were not believers in Christ at this time. As these are brought before Christ, they will be separated by their acts toward the remnant of the nation of Israel:

> *And the King shall answer and say unto them, Verily I*
> *say unto you, Inasmuch as ye have done it unto one of the*
> *least of these my brethren, ye have done it unto me* (Matthew 25:40).

At what place in Scripture are people spiritually saved by the works of the flesh? These people are physically saved to enter the millennial reign of Christ on the earth because of their works:

And before him shall be gathered all nations: and he shall separate them one from another, as a shepherd divideth his sheep from the goats:

And he shall set the sheep on his right hand, but the goats on the left.

Then shall the King say unto them on his right hand, Come, ye blessed of my Father, inherit the kingdom prepared for you from the foundation of the world:

For I was an hungered, and ye gave me meat: I was thirsty, and ye gave me drink: I was a stranger, and ye took me in:

Naked, and ye clothed me: I was sick, and ye visited me: I was in prison, and ye came unto me.

Then shall the righteous answer him, saying, Lord, when saw we thee an hungered, and fed thee? or thirsty, and gave thee drink?

When saw we thee a stranger, and took thee in? or naked, and clothed thee?

Or when saw we thee sick, or in prison, and came unto thee?

And the King shall answer and say unto them, Verily I say unto you, Inasmuch as ye have done it unto one of the least of these my brethren, ye have done it unto me (Matthew 25: 32-40).

Those who did not measure up are immediately delivered up for destruction:

And these shall go away into everlasting punishment: but the righteous into life eternal (Matthew 25:46).

The principle view is the determination of who will inhabit the earth as physical human beings; subjects of the reign of the Messiah—Jesus Christ. Those who are unfit will be taken away. (Following the thousand years, some will be translated into spiritual beings.)

In the seventeenth chapter of Luke, we find not only a reference to the days of Noah, but a reference to the days of Lot. Lot was the nephew of Abraham and accompanied him out of the land of their birth, present day Iraq. Lot also gave up idol worship and believed in the God of Abraham. As they multiplied in the promised land, there arose disputes between their herdsmen about grazing rights. Abraham called Lot into council and decided to part ways. Abraham gave Lot the choice of the land he would possess; either the mountain where they offered sacrifice and met with God, or the plain below the mountain. Lot chose the plain and, eventually, the cities of Sodom and Gomorrah.

The story of Noah is the depiction of the deliverance of the Church of the Lord Jesus Christ. The story of Lot is the depiction of the nation of Israel. Both are an example of events at the end of the world:

> *Even as Sodom and Gomorrha, and the cities about them in like manner, giving themselves over to fornication, and going after strange flesh, are set forth for an example, suffering the vengeance of eternal fire* (Jude 1:7).

The nation of Israel rejected their Messiah and moved from the worship of God into the worldly domain and vexed themselves with the concerns of the world though they sat in the gate—a place of honor in the time of Lot.

And delivered just Lot, vexed with the filthy conversation of the wicked:

(For that righteous man dwelling among them, in seeing and hearing, vexed his righteous soul from day to day with their unlawful deed) (2 Peter 2:7-8).

And there came two angels to Sodom at even; and Lot sat in the gate of Sodom: and Lot seeing them rose up to meet them; and he bowed himself with his face toward the ground (Genesis 19:1).

Noah was warned of God to build the ark and entered in at the time of the flood. The door to the ark was closed and sealed by God. The building of the Ark is a picture of the establishment of the body of Christ, the Church. Lot was warned by the angels and delivered out of the city. This will happen to Israel at the Abomination of Desolation, the midpoint of the last seven years.

In both cases the wicked were destroyed. Israel will depart the land of Judah when the abomination of desolation occurs and prior to the destruction of all the armies surrounding Jerusalem.

When ye therefore shall see the abomination of desolation, spoken of by Daniel the prophet, stand in the holy place, (whoso readeth, let him understand:)
Then let them which be in Judaea flee into the mountains: (Matthew 24:15-16).

Not all of the nation of Israel will escape.

Remember Lot's wife. (Luke 17:32)

According to the Scripture, only one-third of the nation of Israel will escape. The Jewish people have prospered in the world and many will choose not to lose their material possessions. Aspiring to survive the reign of the Antichrist, they will trust in their wealth only to find destruction.

Christ isn't coming to take the believer away, but to establish a kingdom in which we will be joint heirs by our faith in Him.

The Harvest

I can't explain the reasoning behind those who are proponents of the theories of a pre- and mid-tribulation catching away. They disavow the teachings of Christ on the events of His return.

> *Let both grow together until the harvest: and in the time of harvest I will say to the reapers, Gather ye together first the tares, and bind them in bundles to burn them: but gather the wheat into my barn* (Matthew 13:30).

This scripture is directly contrary to the teaching that the believers will first be taken away. The harvest only comes in the fullness of time, when the crop is ripe, and the tares are harvested first.

Ruth and Boaz

The story of Ruth and Boaz is a story about the Bride, the Church, depicted by Ruth. Ruth was not of the nation of Israel and neither are we, but we are all descendants of Adam. Boaz represents Christ, a kinsman redeemer. Their marriage takes place after the harvest on the threshing floor which represents the tribulation. The tares will be gathered and burned and the chaff will be separated from the wheat. The chaff represents the worldliness in our lives and the good grain represents the believers after the worldliness has been removed from us. The tares represent the unbeliever:

Every man's work shall be made manifest: for the day shall declare it, because it shall be revealed by fire; and the fire shall try every man's work of what sort it is.

If any man's work abide which he hath built thereupon, he shall receive a reward.

If any man's work shall be burned, he shall suffer loss: but he himself shall be saved; yet so as by fire (1 Corinthians 3:13-15).

The field is the world; the good seed are the children of the kingdom; but the tares are the children of the wicked one;

The enemy that sowed them is the devil; the harvest is the end of the world; and the reapers are the angels.

As therefore the tares are gathered and burned in the fire; so shall it be in the end of this world.

The Son of man shall send forth his angels, and they shall gather out of his kingdom all things that offend, and them which do iniquity;

And shall cast them into a furnace of fire: there shall be wailing and gnashing of teeth.

Then shall the righteous shine forth as the sun in the kingdom of their Father. Who hath ears to hear, let him hear (Matthew 13:38-43).

CHAPTER 7

THE RAPTURE

The word *rapture* is not found in the Bible. Webster's definition is, "1. The state of being carried away with joy, love. etc.; ecstasy. 2. An expression of great joy, pleasure, etc.; 3. (rare) A carrying away or being carried away in body or spirit."

Who knows who the first person was to use this word in association with the description of an event written about by the Apostle Paul. Over the years, its meaning in religious circles has come to be known as: being taken from the earth by Christ at any moment prior to an event called the tribulation. At the appearance of Christ, there will be rapture, a great joy, ecstasy and a mysterious metamorphosis of all the living human beings who have professed their faith in Christ as the begotten Son of God; or more directly, as God Himself in the form of man:

> *In the beginning was the Word, and the Word was with God, and the Word was God* (John 1:1).

> *And the Word was made flesh, and dwelt among us, (and we beheld his glory, the glory as of the only begotten of the Father,) full of grace and truth* (John 1:14).

This changing, with an added expulsion from the earth, is what is commonly called the rapture:

> *Behold, I show you a mystery; We shall not all sleep, but we shall all be changed, In a moment, in the twinkling of an eye, at the last trump* (1 Corinthians 15:51-52).

It seems that a problem arises concerning the attempt by some to place a distinction on the redeemed of the earth:

❏ Those that believed before the Church was established.

❏ Those that believed and received salvation after the death, burial and resurrection of Jesus Christ.

❏ Those who will be redeemed during the Great Tribulation.

To show this distinction, they have Christ catching away only those redeemed during the Church age. That leaves the difficult task of deciding when and where the rest will be resurrected and glorified, and what place they will occupy in the plan of the ages.

There is, and always has been, only one way of salvation from eternal damnation. Those before Christ believed that God would send a lamb—Christ—to be the sacrifice for their sins. They exhibited this faith by offerings of animals. It pictured their belief of the death of a redeemer. They were saved by their faith looking forward to Christ. Those after Christ believed that He was the Redeemer and, thus, were saved by looking back to His finished work on the cross. They exhibit their faith by trying to attain a lifestyle that conforms to the teaching of Christ. To help Christians in their conformation, he sent the third person of the Trinity, the Holy Spirit. The Trinity is the Father, the Son and the Holy Spirit. Those saved during the tribulation will also be saved by faith in Jesus Christ's atonement.

For whom he did foreknow, he also did predestinate to be conformed to the image of his Son, that he might be the firstborn among many brethren (Romans 8:29).

In the kingdom of God, there will not be Old Testament believers, New Testament believers or Tribulation believers. In the kingdom of God, there will only be believers who trust in the substitution death of the Lord Jesus Christ. All believers who have died in the history of the world are the *dead in Christ*:

For as in Adam all die, even so in Christ shall all be made alive (1 Corinthians 15:22).

For the Lord himself shall descend from heaven with a shout, with the voice of the archangel, and with the trump of God: and the dead in Christ shall rise first:

67

> *Then we which are alive and remain shall be caught up together with them in the clouds, to meet the Lord in the air: and so shall we ever be with the Lord* (1 Thessalonians4:16 -17).

Meeting the Lord in the air is a far cry from being taken anywhere. We need to be careful that we do not add to the Scriptures, so that they agree with our point of view. The Word of God does not contradict itself, unless we make it contradict itself. The wicked will be taken away, the righteous will be resurrected and changed. Those in-between, the unsaved who still rejected the Antichrist and his mark, will populate the restored earth.

CHAPTER 8

THE MESSAGE
OF THE CYCLES

Seventy weeks are determined upon thy people and upon thy holy city, to finish the transgression, and to make an end of sins, and to make reconciliation for iniquity, and to bring in everlasting righteousness, and to seal up the vision and prophecy, and to anoint the most Holy.

Know therefore and understand, that from the going forth of the commandment to restore and to build Jerusalem unto the Messiah the Prince shall be seven weeks, and threescore and two weeks: the street shall be built again, and the wall, even in troublous times.

And after threescore and two weeks shall Messiah be cut off, but not for himself: and the people of the prince that shall come shall destroy the city and the sanctuary; and the end thereof shall be with a flood, and unto the end of the war desolations are determined.

And he shall confirm the covenant with many for one week: and in the midst of the week he shall cause the sacrifice and the oblation to cease, and for the over spreading of abominations he shall make it desolate, even until the consummation, and that determined shall be poured upon the desolate (Daniel 9:24-27).

In the ninth chapter of the book of Daniel, beginning with verse twenty-four and following through verse twenty-seven, we read about the angel Gabriel who came to the prophet Daniel and explained the prophecy and the visions about the end of the age.

A question I am often asked concerns the location of the scripture referring to a final seven year period in earth's history. The answer to that question has its roots in the book of Daniel.

Seventy weeks are determined upon thy people and upon thy holy city, to finish the transgression, and to make an end of sins, and to make reconciliation for iniquity, and to bring in everlasting righteousness, and to seal up the vision and prophecy, and to anoint the most Holy (Daniel 9:24).

In verse twenty-four we find the term *seventy weeks*. If we take this literally, we find that seventy weeks means 490 days. This would mean that 490 days after Daniel received the interpretation of the vision, the Lord Jesus would come and be anointed king. *"To bring in everlasting righteousness, and to seal up the vision and prophecy, and to anoint the most Holy."* We know, only by looking back in history, that this was not the case. We know that this was to be a period of a least 490 years, with an interval period of grace.

In Daniel 9:25, this period of the 490 years is broken down into three portions.

The *seven weeks* was the length of time it took to rebuild the wall around the city of Jerusalem. *Three score and two weeks* was the length of time it took the people to make the city inhabitable. We know that the commandment to restore the wall of Jerusalem was given on the fourteenth day, in the month Nissan, 445 B.C. This is found in Nehemiah 2:1. The decree was issued by the Persian King, Artaxerxes Longimanus.

It took the people 49 years to restore the wall: seven weeks of seven years.

The second portion of time is the 434 years it took to make the city inhabitable; 62 weeks of years—a week of days is seven days, a week of years is seven years:

$$7x7=49 \text{ years} \qquad 62x7=434 \text{ years}$$

When added together this equals 69 weeks of years, or 483 years. This accounts for all but seven years of the interpretation given by Gabriel.

We know for a fact that the Messiah's death came at the end of this 483 years, to the day. It was on the sixth day of Nissan, 32 B.C., that the Lord was crucified. *This was Passover.*

There is no discrepancy in years, when we understand that the prophetic lunar year contained only 360 days, while our solar year contains 365.25 days. There is only one year from 1 B.C. to 1 A.D.; not two years.

$$483 \text{ x } 360 = 173,880 \text{ days.}$$
173,880 divided by 365.25 will give you the correct number of years.

71

Because we have the luxury of looking back, we can see how the remaining portion of Scripture can be interpreted:

> *And after threescore and two weeks shall Messiah be cut off, but not for himself: and the people of the prince that shall come shall destroy the city and the sanctuary; and the end thereof shall be with a flood, and unto the end of the war desolations are determined* (Daniel 9:26).

In exactly 483 years, the Messiah was crucified. It took an additional 36 years for the Romans to destroy the city. This was done by Titus in the year 70 A.D. So, we can see from our viewpoint in history that there was a break of at least thirty-six years between the 69th week of years and the 70th week of years.

(Figure 1. The first 483 years separated by the church age from the final 7 years of the prophecy of Daniel. This break has lasted for a period of about two thousand years.)

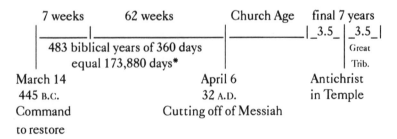

```
        69 weeks of years                      70th week
|_____|  2000 years  |_____|
     69 weeks x 7 = 483 years                7 years    2007
```

(Figure 2. The division of the final 7 years)

```
     7 weeks        62 weeks         Church Age    final 7 years
    |_____|_____|   _____| |_3.5_|_3.5_|
       483 biblical years of 360 days              Great
           equal 173,880 days*                      Trib.
March 14                      April 6           Antichrist
445 B.C.                      32 A.D.           in Temple
Command               Cutting off of Messiah
to restore
```

(The calculation of dates are from the Royal Observatory, Greenwich, United Kingdom. *Calculations include leap year days 116 plus the number of days from March 14 to April 6 (24). A total of 140 additional days.)

The flood, wars and desolations (Daniel 9:26) can very well depict the world in which we have lived for the last 2000 years. We can also take a look and see that Daniel chapter nine verse twenty-four has not been fulfilled. There have been no end to transgressions. There has been no end to sin; no reconciliation for iniquities. Everlasting righteousness has not been brought in. The visions and prophecies have not been sealed up and Jesus has not been anointed the Most Holy.

It remains, therefore, that there is a time when the remaining week will begin and all these things will come to a conclusion. That, my friend, is where all those preachers get that seven years that they are always preaching and writing about.

That brings us to verse twenty-seven: the final seven years of the history of this age.

And he shall confirm the covenant with many for one week: (seven years) and in the midst of the week (three and one-half years) he shall cause the sacrifice and the oblation to cease, and for the over spreading of abominations he shall make it desolate, even until the consummation, and that determined shall be poured upon the desolate (Daniel 9:27).

The confirmation of a covenant will begin this last period of years and it will be strengthened by the Antichrist.

This confirmation will be for seven years and, in the middle of the seven years this confirmation will be broken when the Antichrist enters the rebuilt temple in Jerusalem. The Scriptures say he will cause the sacrifice and oblation to cease. It stands to reason, that the temple of the Jews must be built prior to the middle of this seven years, but not necessarily before the last seven years begins. This temple could have its origin during the first three and one-half years of the last seven.

The word *confirm* in verse twenty-seven shows that the Antichrist will not make the treaty, but will strengthen the treaty. *Confirm* in Hebrew is:

Gabar, gaw-bar'...to prevail, act insolently:—exceed, confirm, be great, be mighty, prevail, put to more [strength], strengthen, be stronger, be valiant.

This covenant will be with *many*.

I have always thought, as do most, that this indicated a large group of people or nations. If that were true, it would contradict the prophecy of the Apostle John who saw a ten-nation confederacy called, "the Beast"; ruled over at the beginning by ten kings and then reduced to eight:

And there are seven kings: five are fallen, and one is, and the other is not yet come; and when he cometh, he must continue a short space.

And the beast that was, and is not, even he is the eighth, and is of the seven, and goeth into perdition.

And the ten horns which thou sawest are ten kings, which have received no kingdom as yet; but receive power as kings one hour with the beast (Revelation 17:10-12).

There is also confirmation in Daniel that three of the ten kings will be destroyed by the rise of the Antichrist:

I considered the horns, and, behold, there came up among them another little horn, before whom there were three of the first horns plucked up by the roots: and, behold, in this horn were eyes like the eyes of man, and a mouth speaking great things (Daniel 7:8).

I'm not sure that you could consider *ten* as being many, but we have another clue. The word *many* translated into Hebrew is *Rab*, and could mean *captain*:

Rab; abundant (in quantity, size, age, number, rank, quality):—(in) abound (-undance, -ant, -antly), captain, elder, enough, exceedingly, full, great (-ly, man, one), increase, many, master, mighty, more, (too, very) much, multiply (-tude), officer, often, plenteous, populous, prince, process.

It's possible that it's the name or position of a man who signs a treaty on behalf of the nation of Israel. I suppose it was just a coincidence that the prime minister of Israel was *Rab*ine, when a treaty for seven years was signed on September 13, 1993; the day of the Feast of Tabernacles.

At the death of Rabine, all Heads of State met to confirm this treaty. The treaty signed was between Yassar Arafat and Rabine, the prime minister of Israel. President Clinton just affirmed the treaty as the president of the United States. I wonder what was contained in that treaty, what promises were made? As of this date, none of the treaty has been publicly broadcast. It's a possibility that only time will reveal the truth.

CHAPTER 9

IMMINENCE

T he pre-tribulation position bases a large portion of its
assumptions on the thought of the return of Christ at
any time,. It is their conclusion based on the scriptural references of Christ returning as a thief.

> *Behold, I come as a thief. Blessed is he that watcheth,
> and keepeth his garments, lest he walk naked, and they see
> his shame* (Revelation 6:15).

> *Remember therefore how thou hast received and heard,
> and hold fast, and repent. If therefore thou shalt not watch,
> I will come on thee as a thief, and thou shalt not know what
> hour I will come upon thee* (Revelation 3:3).

From these, and two other references (Matthew 24:43
& Luke 12:39), the doctrine of imminence becomes the
pier of the pre-tribulation foundation. The question is this:

can Jesus Christ return at any time without any further fulfillment of prophetic scripture? This teaching has its strong points concerning the conduct of the people of God. The proponents believe that the fear of the unannounced return of the Lord will cause us to maintain good works. However, it doesn't say much about the faith, love and abiding of the Holy Spirit in the lives of the believers. Do we serve God and try to live Christ-like out of fear? I like the definition of the word *free* in the Greek:

Eleutheros: unrestrained (to go at pleasure) i.e. (as a citizen) not a slave, or exempt (from obligation or liability).

Those whom the Lord hath made free, are free indeed:

There is no fear in love; but perfect love casteth out fear: because fear hath torment. He that feareth is not made perfect in love (1 John 4:18).

It's the same old story; making a doctrine out of a few verses taken out of context. The Scripture is not of private interpretation. This, then, is the meaning: a person must examine the whole text of the Bible concerning a particular subject to get the true doctrine on that subject.

The phrase *as a thief*, occurs six times in the New Testament. Twice it refers to Christ returning as a thief (Revelation 3:3; 16:15); three times it refers to the Day of the Lord coming as a thief (1 Thessalonians 5:2, 5:4 & 2 Peter 3:10); and once refers to the believers not suffering as a thief (1 Peter 4:5). The Day of the Lord and the return of Christ are the same event.

78

The pre-tribulation rapture supporters will not accept this because they know that the Day of the Lord occurs at the end of the tribulation. An admission to this fact would necessarily destroy their belief in imminence. Could Christ return at any time? Not according to Daniel. Daniel prophesied the birth, death and the establishment of the Messiah as king. While it's true, he didn't view the ages of the Church, it does not destroy the truth of what he did know. Daniel knew from the vision that the remainder of all time has been divided into seven year increments, regardless of the amount of time of the Church.

Furthermore, he knew that all of time would be divided into *jubilees*, an event that occurred every fifty years, with the fiftieth year being the first year of the next fifty. Therefore, we lose ten years out of five hundred. A person would count forty-nine years and the next year counted both, one and fifty.

$$1\ 2\ 3 - 49\ 50$$
$$1\ 2\ 3 - 49\ 50$$
$$1\ 2\ 3 - \text{etc.}$$

What Daniel knew was that the Lord would die at the end of a seven year cycle. From the commandment to restore and rebuild Jerusalem, 69 weeks of years (69 x7 = 483 years). Christ would be anointed King at the end of a seven year cycle on a jubilee year (70 x 7 = 490 years from the same date, minus the Church ages). Christ cannot appear except on the Jubilee.

And ye shall hallow the fiftieth year, and proclaim liberty throughout all the land unto all the inhabitants thereof:

it shall be a jubilee unto you; and ye shall return every man unto his possession, and ye shall return every man unto his family (Leviticus 25:10).

The jubilee would have been 2,520 days after the death of Christ in 32 A.D. From that time there would have been a jubilee every 17,640 days.

If you care to calculate:

7 years at 360 days per year = 2,520 days
2,520 days multiplied by seven would be a jubilee, which would be 17,640 days.

The Royal Observatory, Greenwich, is just one of many who seek to place dates to historical events. These estimates range from 1998 to 2012. I am not attempting to set a date for the year of Jubilee. My attempt is to show that the event is predated by at least seven years with the building of the temple in Jerusalem. When we see the building of the temple, then we look for the revealing of the Antichrist. I believe we can be relatively sure that we are nearing a Jubilee date shortly after the year 2000.

The main point is this: if Christ's kingdom is only established at the jubilee year that occurs at only fifty year increments, then, even from a pre- mid- or post-tribulation rapture persuasion, Christ could only come one day in a seven year period prior to the jubilee; which would still only be one day out of fifty years.

Consider this: If your life is less than 100 years, then there will be only two opportunities for Christ to return in your life time.

The Feast's

There were seven feasts that God established for the people to observe: Passover, Unleavened Bread, Firstfruits, Feast of Weeks (Pentecost), Trumpets, Day of Atonement, and Feast of Tabernacles. The Apostle Paul describes how three of these were atypical to the redemptive work of Christ:

> *Purge out therefore the old leaven, that ye may be a new lump, as ye are unleavened. For even Christ our passover is sacrificed for us:*
> *Therefore let us keep the feast, not with old leaven, neither with the leaven of malice and wickedness; but with the unleavened bread of sincerity and truth* (1 Corinthians 5:7-8).
> *But now is Christ risen from the dead, and become the firstfruits of them that slept* (1 Corinthians 15:20).

Pentecost was the day which the Church was given the gift of the baptism of the Holy Spirit:

> *But this is that which was spoken by the prophet Joel;*
> *And it shall come to pass in the last days, saith God, I will pour out of my Spirit upon all flesh: and your sons and your daughters shall prophesy, and your young men shall see visions, and your old men shall dream dreams* (Acts 2:16-17).

If the first four feast days were prophetic and a fulfillment occurred in the life of Christ and the Church, on the exact day and month, do you not think that the other three will have a literal fulfillment in the future at the return of

Christ? The final feasts occured in the seventh month which is our September. Between Passover and the feast of Trumpets was the time allowed for the crops to grow, ripen and come to harvest. The sound of the trumpet on the Feast of Trumpets was the call to the harvest. The only grain to be harvested prior to this time was the sheaf of firstfruits, and we know from Scripture that this was fulfilled in Christ. Those that preach pre-tribulation and mid-tribulation deny the scriptural teaching of the harvest and the gleanings—(the kingdom inhabitants changed at the end of the thousand years).

> *And when the thousand years are expired, Satan shall be loosed out of his prison,*
> *And shall go out to deceive the nations which are in the four quarters of the earth, Gog and Magog, to gather them together to battle: the number of whom is as the sand of the sea.*
> *And they went up on the breadth of the earth, and compassed the camp of the saints about, and the beloved city: and fire came down from God out of heaven, and devoured them.*
> *And the devil that deceived them was cast into the lake of fire and brimstone, where the beast and the false prophet are, and shall be tormented day and night for ever and ever* (Revelation 20:7-10).

> *And death and hell were cast into the lake of fire. This is the second death* (Revelation 20:14).

> *Then cometh the end, when he shall have delivered up the kingdom to God, even the Father; when he shall have put down all rule and all authority and power.*

For he must reign, till he hath put all enemies under his feet.

The last enemy that shall be destroyed is death.

For he hath put all things under his feet. But when he saith all things are put under him, it is manifest that he is excepted, which did put all things under him.

And when all things shall be subdued unto him, then shall the Son also himself be subject unto him that put all things under him, that God may be all in all (1 Corinthians 15:24-28).

The kingdom which Christ delivers up is the earthly, one-thousand-year kingdom. It would not make sense to deliver up a spiritual kingdom to become a spiritual kingdom. In the Scriptures, the kingdom of heaven is not the same as the kingdom of God. When Christ spoke about the kingdom of heaven, He was speaking about His earthly rule over a restored nation of Israel. The proof is in the next chapter.

CHAPTER 10

THE WEDDING FEAST

The kingdom of heaven is like unto a certain king, which made a marriage for his son,
And sent forth his servants to call them that were bidden to the wedding: and they would not come (Matthew 22:2-3).

Then saith he to his servants, The wedding is ready, but they which were bidden were not worthy.
Go ye therefore into the highways, and as many as ye shall find, bid to the marriage.
So those servants went out into the highways, and gathered together all as many as they found, both bad and good: and the wedding was furnished with guests (Matthew 22:8-10).

Many preachers have stood in the pulpit and preached this text. Invariably, those that were bidden to come to the marriage are the lost; and those that seek someone to invite to the marriage are the righteous trying to save the lost!

The kingdom of heaven is like this. Those who belong to Christ are the Bride, the king is God the father and the Son is Christ Jesus. The millennial reign of Christ will be the marriage and marriage supper. Of the humans left after the tribulation warfare, some will be the invited guests. The Bride is not the invited guest to her own wedding. We can be sure there are at least three persons in this parable who will be at the ceremony; the Father, the Son and the Bride. When Christ appeared the first time, it was to invite the nation of Israel. This invitation was rejected, so during the tribulation there will be an attempt to populate the wedding with anyone who will come. Those from the highways and byways will be gathered for the wedding feast, but not all will be allowed to attend:

> *And when the king came in to see the guests, he saw there a man which had not on a wedding garment:*
>
> *And he saith unto him, Friend, how camest thou in hither not having a wedding garment? And he was speechless.*
>
> *Then said the king to the servants, Bind him hand and foot, and take him away, and cast him into outer darkness; there shall be weeping and gnashing of teeth.*
>
> *For many are called, but few are chosen* (Matthew 22:11-14).

Again, this is not the Bride. The guests are checked for the right garments. In this case, it is the good works they have done during the tribulation that accounts for being welcomed:

> *And the King shall answer and say unto them, Verily I say unto you, Inasmuch as ye have done it unto one of the least of these my brethren, ye have done it unto me* (Matthew 25:40).

There is another passage of Scripture that many preachers stay away from along these same lines:

> *Then shall the kingdom of heaven be likened unto ten virgins, which took their lamps, and went forth to meet the bridegroom.*
> *And five of them were wise, and five were foolish.*
> *They that were foolish took their lamps, and took no oil with them:*
> *But the wise took oil in their vessels with their lamps.*
> *While the bridegroom tarried, they all slumbered and slept.*
> *And at midnight there was a cry made, Behold, the bridegroom cometh; go ye out to meet him.*
> *Then all those virgins arose, and trimmed their lamps.*
> *And the foolish said unto the wise, Give us of your oil; for our lamps are gone out.*
> *But the wise answered, saying, Not so; lest there be not enough for us and you: but go ye rather to them that sell, and buy for yourselves.*
> *And while they went to buy, the bridegroom came; and they that were ready went in with him to the marriage: and the door was shut.*

> *Afterward came also the other virgins, saying, Lord, Lord, open to us.*
> *But he answered and said, Verily I say unto you, I know you not.*
> *Watch therefore, for ye know neither the day nor the hour wherein the Son of man cometh* (Matthew 25:1-13).

If this parable were about the Church, there would have been only one virgin and the reference would have been, *"the bride slept."* In the world of the Israelis and at the time of this teaching, marriages were negotiated. The parties involved often had no say about who their mates would be. This is also true of the Church:

> *In whom also we have obtained an inheritance, being predestinated according to the purpose of him who worketh all things after the counsel of his own will* (Ephesians 1:11).

> *According as he hath chosen us in him before the foundation of the world, that we should be holy and without blame before him in love* (Ephesians 1:4).

It is evident that the marriage of the believers to Christ was negotiated before the event was to take place. Therefore, the ten virgins must be some other group of people.

The Mixed Multitude

The story of Israel in the land of Egypt is: plagues, oppression for their religion, and going to the promised land. This is a story of the return of the Christ. Israel was led by a deliverer, Moses—a symbol of the Lord. But, they were not all Israel. Some of the Egyptians had come to believe in the God of Israel. When the people of Israel left Egypt. they followed along:

> *And a mixed multitude went up also with them* (Exodus 12:38).

When Christ returns to the earth, the events will take place in a sequential manner. First, those who have died believing that God would send Christ and did send Christ— Old Testament, Church, and Tribulation believers. These who have died in their faith, their bodies will be resurrected from the earth:

> *For the Lord himself shall descend from heaven with a shout, with the voice of the archangel, and with the trump of God: and the dead in Christ shall rise first* (1 Thessalonians 4:16).

These bodies will be reunited with their eternal soul and spirit that have been in the keeping of God:

> *Then shall the dust return to the earth as it was: and the spirit shall return unto God who gave it* (Ecclesiastes 12:7).

> *And when he had opened the fifth seal, I saw under the altar the souls of them that were slain for the Word of God, and for the testimony which they held* (Revelation 6:9).

The spirit and the soul will be joined at the resurrection to the bodies that have been changed from corruptible to incorruptible:

> *For this corruptible must put on incorruption, and this mortal must put on immortality.*
>
> *So when this corruptible shall have put on incorruption, and this mortal shall have put on immortality, then shall be brought to pass the saying that is written, Death is swallowed up in victory* (1 Corinthians 15:53).

The next event will be the translation (rapture) of those believers that survived the Great Tribulation. It must be noted that although Israel believes the Messiah is coming, they will not believe that Jesus Christ, the son of Mary of Bethlehem—is the Messiah until He returns. These events happen prior to their recognition that their long-awaited Messiah is none other than Jesus:

> *Behold, he cometh with clouds; and every eye shall see him, and they also which pierced him: and all kindreds of the earth shall wail because of him. Even so, Amen* (Revelation 1:7).

> *And again another scripture saith, They shall look on him whom they pierced* (John 19:37).

The translation of living believers follows the resurrection. This is most important and a key to the correct doctrine concerning the timing of the translation—the rapture:

*In a moment, in the twinkling of an eye, at the last
trump: for (1) the trumpet shall sound, and (2) the dead
shall be raised incorruptible, and (3) we shall be changed*
(1 Corinthians 15:52).

Next, the people who survived the tribulation not believing that Jesus was the Messiah, yet believing the message that there was a Messiah and that He would set up a
kingdom on the earth, will enter into that thousand year
kingdom. This is the mixed multitude, the same as those
who left Egypt after the plagues fell upon that land. They
did not follow the pharaoh as in the future there will be
some who will not follow the Antichrist.

*For unto us was the gospel preached, as well as unto
them: but the word preached did not profit them, not being mixed with faith in them that heard it* (Hebrews 4:2).

Of this mixed multitude that did not trust in Jesus, yet
did not worship the Antichrist or receive his mark on their
hand or forehead, some will be rejected. It is because they
did not act on faith. Though they are considered virgins
(those who reject both the Antichrist and Jesus Christ),
they have no *oil* in their lamps, the Holy Spirit. The lamp
is their life; what they are inside that causes a person to act
out what they really feel. In this regard, the adornment
(their works) is the result of their true feelings.

The ones found with acceptable garments are the guests
at the marriage of the Lamb—Jesus—to the Bride—the
Church; a thousand years of celebration.

CHAPTER 11

THE RESURRECTIONS— HOW MANY AND WHEN?

The greatest key to end-time events is the order of the resurrections and the number. This has been the most overlooked repudiation of the pre- and mid-tribulation doctrine. The pre-tribulationists teach four resurrections:

1) The resurrection of Christ (the Firstfruits).

2) The pre-tribulation resurrection of the dead in Christ.

3) The post-tribulation resurrection of those who believe in Jesus during the tribulation, including Old Testament believers.

4) The post-millennial resurrection of all those who died in unbelief—the lost, unredeemed sinners. The resurrection at the Great White Throne.

The mid-tribulationist teach four resurrections:

1) The resurrection of Christ (the Firstfruits).
2) The mid-tribulation resurrection of the dead in Christ.
3-4) Same as pre-tribulation.

As you can see, the only differences are their views on the resurrection of the dead in Christ. They arrive at their conclusions based on two passages (Matthew 24 & 1 Thessalonians 2). Both of these passages teach that the abomination of desolation must take place before the return of Christ for the elect. The question is, *how many resurrections?*

There are three scriptures in the whole Bible that tell the number of resurrections of people; and there is one that tells the number of resurrections of Christ, plus the believers. I will visit each of these in this chapter:

And many of them that sleep in the dust of the earth shall awake, some to everlasting life, and some to shame and everlasting contempt (Daniel 12:2).

At first look, a person might think that this passage is speaking of only one resurrection. That is why we need to examine the whole Word of God to exact the truth. It is evident that there are only two groups of people mentioned in this scripture. There is the group that will awake to everlasting life, and the group that shall awake to shame and contempt:

Marvel not at this: for the hour is coming, in the which all that are in the graves shall hear his voice,

And shall come forth; they that have done good, unto the resurrection of life; and they that have done evil, unto the resurrection of damnation (John 5:28-29).

The picture becomes just a little clearer in this portion of Scripture. The word *resurrection* is used twice which would indicate two distinct events. We still have two groups of people. If, in this scripture, only one event was in view, I doubt that it would have been worded in this manner. More than likely, it would have been similar to that found in Daniel. Just to assure you that there are two events depicted here, I introduce this scripture:

And I saw thrones, and they sat upon them, and judgment was given unto them: and I saw the souls of them that were beheaded for the witness of Jesus, and for the word of God, and which had not worshipped the beast, neither his image, neither had received his mark upon their foreheads, or in their hands; and they lived and reigned with Christ a thousand years.

But the rest of the dead lived not again until the thousand years were finished. This is the first resurrection (Revelation 20:4-5).

Every preacher I've ever heard has preached that we will sit in judgment:

Do ye not know that the saints shall judge the world? and if the world shall be judged by you, are ye unworthy to judge the smallest matters?

Know ye not that we shall judge angels? how much more things that pertain to this life? (1 Corinthians 6:2-3).

> *And Enoch also, the seventh from Adam, prophesied of these, saying, Behold, the Lord cometh with ten thousands of his saints,*
> *To execute judgment upon all* (Jude 1:14-15).

I have also heard hundreds preach that we shall live and reign with Christ:

> *If we suffer, we shall also reign with him: if we deny him, he also will deny us* (2 Tim 2:12).

> *And hast made us unto our God kings and priests: and we shall reign on the earth* (Revelation 5:10).

> *Blessed and holy is he that hath part in the first resurrection: on such the second death hath no power, but they shall be priests of God and of Christ, and shall reign with him a thousand years* (Revelation 20:6).

> *And there shall be no night there; and they need no candle, neither light of the sun; for the Lord God giveth them light: and they shall reign for ever and ever (Revelation 22:5).*

It seems they like the part about ruling, reigning and judging. They reject the part about having to be subjected to the mark of the beast. According to their position we're supposed to be gone when this happens. Their doctrine is just torn to shreds at the insinuation that the first resurrection takes place after the issuance of the mark of the beast. Surely, they believe there is some explanation when the Scriptures say that this is the first resurrection. It's like taking what you like and rejecting the rest. This is the first resurrection of the world as a whole; the resurrection of the good, the resurrection of life and the ones who will receive eternal life.

There were seven resurrections of people who would eventually die again:
1) The son of the widow of Zarephath (1 Kings 17:22).
2) The son of the Shunammite woman (2 Kings 4:35).
3) The dead man restored to life at the touch of Elisha's bones (2 Kings 13:21).
4) Jarius' daughter (Matthew 9:25).
5) The son of the widow of Nain (Luke 7:15).
6) Lazarus of Bethany (John 11:44).
7) Dorcas (Acts 9:40).

These are not regarded as first resurrections according to the passage of Scripture in Revelation.

Firstfruits

The resurrection of Christ, as mentioned in earlier chapters, was the resurrection of the Firstfruits. Some may think I have missed the resurrection of the saints at the time of the resurrection of Christ, but these are the same.

When you plant one seed of grain, you get a plant with many grains on one stalk. Christ was the Seed that died in planting. When He was reaped as the Firstfruits, there had to be more than one grain presented to represent the harvest:

> *And the graves were opened; and many bodies of the saints which slept arose,*

97

> *And came out of the graves after his resurrection, and went into the holy city, and appeared unto many* (Matthew 27:52).

Therefore, Christ and these saints represent the Firstfruits. I would like you to notice that Scripture calls these *saints*. This really throws a kink into the idea that only New Testament believers are called Saints.

It's like I mentioned earlier, there are only two types of people: those who have placed their faith in Christ and those who haven't; those who have done good and those who have done evil. There are only two resurrections of all in the graves. This is what we are dealing with here, and we now know that these two are separated by a period of one thousand years:

> *And they lived and reigned with Christ a thousand years.*
> *But the rest of the dead lived not again until the thousand years were finished* (Revelation 20:4-5).

The Apostle Paul made this very clear when speaking of the resurrection of believers:

> *But now is Christ risen from the dead, and become the firstfruits of them that slept.*
> *For since by man came death, by man came also the resurrection of the dead.*
> *But every man in his own order: Christ the firstfruits; afterward they that are Christ's at his coming* (1 Corinthians 15:20-23).

Parousia

Paul does not mention a pre- or mid- resurrection of the saints. The word that proves the time of the resurrection of Christ's chosen is the word *coming*. In the Greek, it is defined, thus:

Coming .... parousia, par-oo-see'-ah; a being near, i.e. advent (often, return; spec. of Christ to punish Jerusalem, or finally the wicked); (by impl.) phys. aspect:—coming, presence.

Let us examine that word *parousia* in scriptural context. The word is found four times in the twenty-fourth chapter of Matthew. This book and chapter is literally thrown out by the pre-tribulationist. Their conclusion is that Christ is only speaking to the nation of Israel and not the Church.

Why?

It destroys their doctrine if there is evidence that the abomination of desolation takes place before the gathering of the elect. If the elect is the Church. The elect is not just the Church but all believers from Adam until now. This, they are determined not to believe.

The same Greek word is used throughout the New Testament for both Old and New Testament believers:

Elect....eklektos, ek-lek-tos'; select; favorite—chosen, elect.

How can someone say that in one instance it means Old Testament believers and, in the next, it means New Testament believers:

> *And he shall send his angels with a great sound of a trumpet, and they shall gather together his elect from the four winds, from one end of heaven to the other* (Matthew 24:31).

> *Put on therefore, as the elect of God, holy and beloved, bowels of mercies, kindness, humbleness of mind, meekness, longsuffering* (Colossians 3:12).

> *Peter, an apostle of Jesus Christ, to the strangers scattered throughout Pontus, Galatia, Cappadocia, Asia, and Bithynia,*
> *Elect according to the foreknowledge of God the Father* (1 Peter 1:1-2).

These instances all use the same word, yet the pretribulation doctrine rejects that Matthew was writing about believers.

> *Immediately after the tribulation of those days shall the sun be darkened, and the moon shall not give her light, and the stars shall fall from heaven, and the powers of the heavens shall be shaken:*
> *And then shall appear the sign of the Son of man in heaven: and then shall all the tribes of the earth mourn, and they shall see the Son of man coming in the clouds of heaven with power and great glory.*
> *And he shall send his angels with a great sound of a trumpet, and they shall gather together his elect from the four winds, from one end of heaven to the other* (Matthew 24:29-31).

The disciples asked Christ to explain the sign of His Coming—parousia. Christ said that the sign of His appearing would be visable after the sun refused to give its light and the moon turned to blood. This is terror to the pre- and mid-tribulationist because it occurs at the very end of the tribulation. This is also found in other books of the Bible:

The sun shall be turned into darkness, and the moon into blood, before that great and notable day of the Lord come (Acts 2:20).

The sun shall be turned into darkness, and the moon into blood, before the great and the terrible day of the Lord come (Joel 2:31).

This really puts a bind on those other doctrines by placing the gathering of the elect at the very door of the Day of the Lord. Now, just to show that Paul taught the same thing, we will examine his use of the word parousia and his explanation of this event:

Now we beseech you, brethren, by the coming of our Lord Jesus Christ, and by our gathering together unto him (2 Thessalonians 2:1).

The word *coming*—parousia—found here in 2 Thessalonians, is the very same word found in 1 Corinthians 15, and in Matthew 24:

But every man in his own order: Christ the firstfruits; afterward they that are Christ's at his coming (1 Corinthians 15:23).

> *And as he sat upon the mount of Olives, the disciples*
> *came unto him privately, saying, Tell us, when shall these*
> *things be? and what shall be the sign of thy coming, and of*
> *the end of the world* (Matthew 24:3).

It must be apparent that the same event is in view in these three portions of Scripture. Those that teach a pre- or mid-tribulation are adamant that these are not the same event. They also reject the word found in 1 Corinthians by trying to add a resurrection before that written of by the Apostle Paul in 2 Thessalonians. Let's examine it more closely.

Paul wrote that the coming and the gathering would take place at the same time. The plurality of the word *our* was used to indicate an attempt by the writer, Paul, to include himself in this group that was gathered.

Paul knew that he would not be alive when this event would take place:

> *For I think that God hath set forth us the apostles*
> *last, as it were appointed to death: for we are made a*
> *spectacle unto the world, and to angels, and to men* (1
> Corinthians 4:9).

Therefore, whether alive or dead, Paul included himself in this group. When were they going to be with the Lord? When are we going to be with the Lord? You see, we are going at the same time Paul is going because he is in Christ, as all of us that have called upon the Lord for salvation.

There is no record of the time of the writing of the second Epistle to the Thessalonians. Many have placed it as sometime between 49 and 54 A.D. I believe that it was written at a later date, sometime after 70 A.D. In the following commentary, I will explain my reasoning.

Paul, in his writings, mentioned three things that must take place before those that are living will be *raptured*, or translated, and not see death. First, there will be a falling away from the service and worship of God. Second, will be the revealing of the man of sin. Third will be the resurrection of all those that have died through the ages.

> *In a moment, in the twinkling of an eye, at the last trump: for the trumpet shall sound, and the dead shall be raised incorruptible, and we shall be changed* (1 Corinthians 15:52).

> *For this we say unto you by the word of the Lord, that we which are alive and remain unto the coming of the Lord shall not prevent them which are asleep.*
> *For the Lord himself shall descend from heaven with a shout, with the voice of the archangel, and with the trump of God: and the dead in Christ shall rise first* (1 Thessalonians 4:15-16).

Did you notice that word, *coming*, in 1 Thessalonians 4:15? It's the same word as previously mentioned. Same word, same event. We will not prevent those who are dead in their graves. They will be the first to meet the Lord in their glorified bodies. We will be at the twinkling of an eye after.

Preceding the resurrection of the dead is the falling away:

> *Let no man deceive you by any means: for that day*
> *(The day that we are gathered to the Lord) shall not come,*
> *except there come a falling away first, and that man of sin*
> *be revealed, the son of perdition* (2 Thessalonians 2:3).

The word used for the falling away is *apostasy*. In the later days, some will leave the truth of the Word of God for some man-made religion. It will include a perverted version of the Bible.

> Apostasia, ap-os-tas-ee'-ah; defection from truth. ["apostasy"]:—falling away, forsake.

Following the falling away, is the revealing of the man of sin. The revealing of the man of sin is found in the book of Daniel:

> *And he shall confirm the covenant with many for one*
> *week: and in the midst of the week he shall cause the sacri-*
> *fice and the oblation to cease, and for the overspreading of*
> *abominations he shall make it desolate, even until the con-*
> *summation, and that determined shall be poured upon the*
> *desolate* (Daniel 9:27).

This is the event that will reveal the man of sin. It is the same event that Jesus called the abomination of desolation:

> *When ye therefore shall see the abomination of desola-*
> *tion, spoken of by Daniel the prophet, stand in the holy*
> *place, (whoso readeth, let him understand:)* (Matthew
> 24:15).

Daniel wrote that the man of sin would cause the sacrifice and oblation to cease. Jesus added to that description, *stand in the holy place*. The Apostle Paul brought it all together:

> *Who opposeth and exalteth himself above all that is called God, or that is worshipped; so that he as God sitteth in the temple of God, showing himself that he is God* (2 Thessalonians 2:4).

He Who Hinders

In the Epistle to the Thessalonians, Paul wrote extensively about the aforementioned event. Following his explanation, he wrote that there was something that was preventing this from happening and that it would continue to prevent it until it was removed or taken out of the way. Most pre-tribulationists have come to believe that this is in reference to the Church or the Holy Spirit. The Greek used in this instance could mean *that thing*, and it takes a bit of imagination to stretch it to mean the Holy Spirit.

I contend that the context of this particular passage indicates Paul was still involved with the subject of the abomination of desolation, and still had the temple in view. The temple had already been destroyed and, therefore, it was impossible for this event to take place. The lack of a temple is still withholding the man of sin from being revealed. Paul made it very clear that this must take place before he was to be gathered unto the Lord. Since the dead are going to meet the Lord first, he will precede those of us who are in the Lord and still alive.

105

> *And now ye know what withholdeth that he might be revealed in his time* (2 Thessalonians 2:6).

The beginning of this verse leads one to believe that there was something that was not previously known. Following this Epistle and the explanation about the man of sin and his being revealed, this is now known.
Lets review:
1) There will be a perversion of the true gospel and many will succumb to its teachings.
2) The temple has to be rebuilt so that the man of sin can be revealed.
3) The abomination of desolation must take place.
4) The dead in Christ are raised first. That means Old Testament, New Testament and tribulation believers, because there is only one way to God.

The order of the resurrections are:
1) Christ (the Firstfruits).
2) Those that are His at His appearing—coming or parousia.
3) The unrighteous dead at the end of one thousand years.

CHAPTER 12

THE UNRIGHTEOUS DEAD

As there were two thieves separated by Jesus Christ, there will be two resurrections. The difference between the participants of these resurrections will be Christ. Following the millennial reign of Christ previously discussed, Satan will be released from the prison that has contained him for the past one thousand years:

> *And I saw an angel come down from heaven, having the key of the bottomless pit and a great chain in his hand.*
> *And he laid hold on the dragon, that old serpent, which is the Devil, and Satan, and bound him a thousand years* (Revelation 20:1-2).

He will be allowed to tempt those that have been born to the remnant of humans that participate in the kingdom of heaven following the Great Tribulation:

> *And cast him into the bottomless pit, and shut him up,*
> *and set a seal upon him, that he should deceive the nations*
> *no more, till the thousand years should be fulfilled: and*
> *after that he must be loosed a little season* (Revelation
> 20:3).

The sad part is that those born during the thousand
years will not be any better at making choices than Adam
was:

> *And when the thousand years are expired, Satan shall*
> *be loosed out of his prison,*
> *And shall go out to deceive the nations which are in the*
> *four quarters of the earth, Gog and Magog, to gather them*
> *together to battle: the number of whom is as the sand of the*
> *sea.*
> *And they went up on the breadth of the earth, and*
> *compassed the camp of the saints about, and the beloved*
> *city: and fire came down from God out of heaven, and*
> *devoured them* (Revelation 20:7-9).

It seems that a great multitude will rebel against God
and His Son. From the Scriptures, we can read that the
inhabitants will offer animal sacrifices during the one thousand years:

> *And it shall come to pass, that every one that is left of*
> *all the nations which came against Jerusalem shall even go*
> *up from year to year to worship the King, the Lord of*
> *hosts, and to keep the feast of tabernacles* (Zechariah
> 14:16).

And the Lord shall be known to Egypt, and the Egyptians shall know the Lord in that day, and shall do sacrifice and oblation; yea, they shall vow a vow unto the Lord, and perform it (Isaiah 19:21).

Yea, every pot in Jerusalem and in Judah shall be holiness unto the Lord of hosts: and all they that sacrifice shall come and take of them, and see therein: and in that day there shall be no more the Canaanite in the house of the Lord of hosts (Zechariah 14:21).

In That Day

In the Old Testament there is a phrase, *in that day*. It means the time of the kingdom of our Lord. All of the references to the sacrifices during that time could mean that they are a type of memorial to the sacrifice made by the Lord. It seems that all those born will see the Lord on His throne. To commemorate His death, they will offer animal sacrifices.

They will be as we are today: religious, but not knowing the true meaning of godliness. The meaning of their actions will be lost to their human minds. In time, they will forget and their young will consider the rituals a burden. A multitude will follow Satan. After the rebellious are destroyed, the final resurrection will take place:

And I saw a great white throne, and him that sat on it, from whose face the earth and the heaven fled away; and there was found no place for them (Revelation 20:11).

The word *them* indicates that the writer (the Apostle John) did not include himself with this group. A rule that I have tried to use in the interpretation of difficult passages is the use of the words: we, us and our to indicate the writer is included with the group. The words: they, them and those are an indication of exclusion from the group.

These that stand before the Great White Throne are those, throughout history, that have rejected the Lord Jesus Christ as the only means of salvation. They will be judged by the eternal Father of Creation. They will be judged by the law because they have not attained mercy. This in itself is condemnation. The word indicates the no flesh shall be justified by the law.

> *Christ is become of no effect unto you, whosoever of you are justified by the law; ye are fallen from grace* (Gal 5:4).

> *But that no man is justified by the law in the sight of God, it is evident: for, The just shall live by faith* (Gal 3:11).

> *And by him all that believe are justified from all things, from which ye could not be justified by the law of Moses* (Acts 13:39).

As these are judged, books will be opened. These books contain all the thoughts and works of every human being; everything said or done...everything. Then, there will be one final book opened which will be the Book of Life. As a person's works are not enough to gain eternal life, neither are they enough to condemn:

Not by works of righteousness which we have done, but according to his mercy he saved us, by the washing of regeneration, and renewing of the Holy Ghost (Acts 13:39).

The final condemnation is that their names are not found in the Book of Life.

And I saw the dead, small and great, stand before God; and the books were opened: and another book was opened, which is the book of life: and the dead were judged out of those things which were written in the books, according to their works (Revelation 20:12).

And whosoever was not found written in the book of life was cast into the lake of fire (Revelation 20:15).

The sad truth is that everyone begins with their name in the Book of Life. Only after their earthly death, without ever placing their faith in God and His Christ, are their names removed from the Book of Life.

He that overcometh, the same shall be clothed in white raiment; and I will not blot out his name out of the book of life, but I will confess his name before my Father, and before his angels (Revelation 3:5).

And if any man shall take away from the words of the book of this prophecy, God shall take away his part out of the book of life, and out of the holy city, and from the things which are written in this book (Revelation 22:19).

The most difficult doctrine for people to accept is the doctrine that teaches salvation apart from works. Works are a product of salvation and it can be said that a man can be identified by the good works that accompany his life.

Salvation comes first. As a new creation in Christ, we are also created for good works:

> *For if Abraham were justified by works, he hath whereof to glory; but not before God.*
> *For what saith the scripture? Abraham believed God, and it was counted unto him for righteousness.*
> *Now to him that worketh is the reward not reckoned of grace, but of debt.*
> *But to him that worketh not, but believeth on him that justifieth the ungodly, his faith is counted for righteousness* (Romans 4:2-5).

> *For we are his workmanship, created in Christ Jesus unto good works, which God hath before ordained that we should walk in them* (Ephesians 2:10).

If our salvation is not a product of good works, then damnation is not a product of bad works. Salvation or damnation is determined by one's choice about Jesus Christ. Is He the Son of the Creator of the universe? There is no proof other than the Bible and the testimony of those who believe. It is wholly by faith. This faith is a product of the Bible and the words written within:

> *So then faith cometh by hearing, and hearing by the word of God* (Romans 10:17).

Judgment

Many Christians believe that they will not have to face judgment. Therefore, they live circumspect lives. All will come to judgment, both the Christian and the lost. The Christian will stand before Jesus Christ at the judgment seat in contrast to the throne judgment of the lost.

According to the grace of God which is given unto me, as a wise masterbuilder, I have laid the foundation, and another buildeth thereon. But let every man take heed how he buildeth thereupon.

For other foundation can no man lay than that is laid, which is Jesus Christ.

Now if any man build upon this foundation gold, silver, precious stones, wood, hay, stubble;

Every man's work shall be made manifest: for the day shall declare it, because it shall be revealed by fire; and the fire shall try every man's work of what sort it is.

If any man's work abide which he hath built thereupon, he shall receive a reward (1 Corinthians 3:10-14).

For we must all appear before the judgment seat of Christ; that every one may receive the things done in his body, according to that he hath done, whether it be good or bad (2 Corinthians 5:10).

Christian can do bad things. It remains that we must account for these bad deeds. The loss of inestimable riches for eternity stands in the balance, because Christ has spoken that there will be rewards for the faithful follower. We cannot, at this time, define what those rewards will be. We can only trust in the promises of the Lord and try to achieve the greater of these gifts to come:

> *But lay up for yourselves treasures in heaven, where*
> *neither moth nor rust doth corrupt, and where thieves do*
> *not break through nor steal:*
> *For where your treasure is, there will your heart be*
> *also* (Matthew 6:20-21).

The judgment of the believers will take place at the beginning of the Millennium, while the judgment of the unbelievers will take place at the end of the Millennium.

There will be great remorse on behalf of those standing at that place; remorse for those things we could have overcome or could have done.

Will you be happy with your retirement?

I work at a blue collar job, in which I pay-in retirement. I sometimes check on the amount that I'll receive when I retire. I don't think that I can live very well on what I have stored away.

Many have paid social security all their lives in hopes they will be able to survive at an elderly age. Instead, they find that they barely have enough to fill their mouths. Do you want to have this type feeling at the beginning of the eternal day?

There is no wonder that the Scriptures indicate that there will be tears shed in that heavenly place:

> *For the Lamb which is in the midst of the throne shall*
> *feed them, and shall lead them unto living fountains of*
> *waters: and God shall wipe away all tears from their eyes*
> (Revelation 7:17).

CHAPTER 13

AS A THIEF

Watch therefore, for ye know neither the day nor the hour wherein the Son of man cometh (Matthew 25:13).

This particular passage of Scripture is the banner for the no-one-can-know-before-the-tribulation believers. It, of course, is primarily taken out of context. This passage is written to the Israelites, because they are the archetype to the ten virgins discussed earlier. This is the ending of that parable.

Jesus is not just the son of God, He is God. The number one factor in becoming a Christian is confessing of this truth:

> *That if thou shalt confess with thy mouth the Lord Jesus, and shalt believe in thine heart that God hath raised him from the dead, thou shalt be saved* (Romans 10:9).

The word *Lord* here is translated, *kurios*; meaning God or supreme authority. He even said that He and the Father are one:

> *Jesus saith unto him, Have I been so long time with you, and yet hast thou not known me, Philip? he that hath seen me hath seen the Father; and how sayest thou then, Show us the Father?*
>
> *Believest thou not that I am in the Father, and the Father in me? the words that I speak unto you I speak not of myself: but the Father that dwelleth in me, he doeth the works* (John 14:9-10).

If Christ was one with the Father, then He must know the Father's plans concerning His earthly ministry. This causes some problems with the interpretation of this passage of Scripture.

> *But of that day and hour knoweth no man, no, not the angels of heaven, but my Father only* (Matthew 24:36).

> *But of that day and that hour knoweth no man, no, not the angels which are in heaven, neither the Son, but the Father* (Mark 13:32).

As you can see, there are two references.

One, indicates that Jesus did not know the day and the hour of the end of the world. Jesus vividly tells the exact events of His return—not the end of the world, which occurs after His earthly ministry.

The Apostles—John, Peter, and Paul—also tell of the events that complete the end of the age. The *day* indicates the Day of the Lord:

> *But ye, brethren, are not in darkness, that that day should overtake you as a thief* (1 Thessalonians 5:4).

Most Christians that are unschooled in the Scriptures, believe that no one can know when the Lord is coming. This scripture contradicts that opinion. The day that is spoken of in this passage is the Day of the Lord, the day of the return of Christ for the Church. Paul says that we are the children of light and, as such, we will not be overtaken.

I outlined in a previous chapter the things that must happen before we are to meet the Lord. As we see these things come to pass, we know that day draws nearer:

> *For yourselves know perfectly that the day of the Lord so cometh as a thief in the night* (1 Thessalonians 5:2).

If we are going to leave the earth seven years prior to the Day of the Lord, then why does Paul make reference to the fact that the Day of the Lord will not overtake us as a thief. It must be clear that the church is going to go through that period of time called the Great Tribulation. The only ones that are going to be overtaken *as by a thief* are the unbelievers, as in the days of Noah and in the days of Lot.

The end of the world, or the passing of the world as we know it, is somewhere in the distant future. It is the event written of by the Apostle Peter in his second Epistle:

> *Looking for and hasting unto the coming of the day of*
> *God, wherein the heavens being on fire shall be dissolved,*
> *and the elements shall melt with fervent heat?*
>
> *Nevertheless we, according to his promise, look for*
> *new heavens and a new earth, wherein dwelleth righteous-*
> *ness* (2 Peter 3:12-13).

This is the day that Jesus referred to as the day that was known only to the Father.

This day is somewhere past the final rebellion, somewhere past the Millennium.

Remember the three-part question?

1) When will these things be
2) What will be the sign of your coming
3) And the end of the world?

The Day of the Lord may well be the end of earthly life for many who are following false doctrine, but it is not the end of the world. Do not be taken unawares.

This book is written to reveal these things to the children of Light. Those that will not heed these words will be overtaken, and those that reject these words will be overtaken. Those that see with spiritual eyes, and hear with spiritual ears will understand and be prepared.

CHAPTER 14

THE TRUMPET

In the book of Matthew, Jesus makes reference to the sounding of the trumpet when the angels gather the elect:

> *And he shall send his angels with a great sound of a trumpet, and they shall gather together his elect from the four winds, from one end of heaven to the other* (Matthew 24:31).

It should also be observed that the Apostle Paul makes mention of a trumpet in his Epistles about the resurrection and the changing of the mortal to the immortal:

> *In a moment, in the twinkling of an eye, at the last trump: for the trumpet shall sound, and the dead shall be raised incorruptible, and we shall be changed* (1 Corinthians 15:52).

For the Lord himself shall descend from heaven with a shout, with the voice of the archangel, and with the trump of God: and the dead in Christ shall rise first (1 Thessalonians 4:16).

The argument has always been that these were not the same event. If they were the same event, then the resurrection and the gathering would have to follow the events described by the prophet Joel, relating to that period of time following the Great Tribulation.

Bible scholars should know that these are the same events spoken of by Jesus in Matthew 24. The sun will refuse to give its light and the moon will turn to blood. Therefore, when both references speak of a sounding trumpet, it should only lead to a stronger conclusion that these are the same event:

Immediately after the tribulation of those days shall the sun be darkened, and the moon shall not give her light, and the stars shall fall from heaven, and the powers of the heavens shall be shaken (Matthew 24:29).

And he shall send his angels with a great sound of a trumpet, and they shall gather together his elect from the four winds, from one end of heaven to the other (Matthew 24:31).

Multitudes, multitudes in the valley of decision: for the day of the Lord is near in the valley of decision.
The sun and the moon shall be darkened, and the stars shall withdraw their shining (Joel 3:14-15).

The sun shall be turned into darkness, and the moon into blood, before that great and notable day of the Lord come (Acts 2:20).

It would seem that Peter also agreed that these events would precede the coming of the Lord, and that it was possible that he would be present when they occurred. The Scriptures indicate that the trumpet mentioned in Matthew and the trumpet in the teachings of Paul are the same. This would then place the resurrection and the translation after the Great Tribulation:

And I saw thrones, and they sat upon them, and judgment was given unto them: and I saw the souls of them that were beheaded for the witness of Jesus, and for the word of God, and which had not worshipped the beast, neither his image, neither had received his mark upon their foreheads, or in their hands; and they lived and reigned with Christ a thousand years.

But the rest of the dead lived not again until the thousand years were finished. This is the first resurrection (Revelation 20:4-5).

CHAPTER 15

THE BEAST

The Beast of Daniel is already here. I make a distinc
tion between the beast, the man, and the Beast, the
final world government.

In the prophecies of Daniel, there were only five world
kingdoms. The first kingdom was the kingdom of the
Babylonians. The second was the Medeo-Persian empire.
The third was the Grecian empire, and the fourth was the
Roman empire.

All of the aforementioned empires fell to conquering
armies with the exception of the Roman empire. The Roman empire continues to this day, according to the prophecy of Daniel. There have been many kings and kingdoms,
but none have controlled the complete known world. As
time has passed, it has become more difficult because the
known world has become the whole world. The Roman
empire has continued, not as a physical location, but, as a
system. The immoral, political and religious influence of

that empire has continued within all of the kingdoms of the world.

The Roman empire will culminate in final form just before the second advent of Jesus Christ:

> *And whereas thou sawest the feet and toes, part of potters' clay, and part of iron, the kingdom shall be divided; but there shall be in it of the strength of the iron, forasmuch as thou sawest the iron mixed with miry clay* (Daniel 2:41).

> *And in the days of these kings shall the God of heaven set up a kingdom, which shall never be destroyed: and the kingdom shall not be left to other people, but it shall break in pieces and consume all these kingdoms, and it shall stand for ever* (Daniel 2:44).

The final form of the fourth world empire will be as the toes of a human statue. Much speculation has been made as to what countries these toes will represent. It may not represent countries at all. The Roman empire has assumed an economic form, because all countries are the Roman empire. We of the United States are a part of the Roman empire. Therefore, these ten toes represent economic regions that cover the globe.

The North American Free Trade Agreement, and the Global Agreement on Trades and Tariffs, are an attempt to consolidate economic areas agreed upon by the World Economic Summit. This group has been called *the G-7* since 1989.

At the summit in 1990, the world was divided into ten regions. All the leaders of the G-7 have devoted their efforts to bringing their plans to fruition. The ten regions are:

1) United States, Canada and Mexico.
2) Western Europe.
3) Japan.
4) Australia and New Zealand.
5) Eastern Europe.
6) Latin America.
7) North Africa and the Middle East.
8) Central Africa.
9) South and southeast Asia.
10) Central Asia.

The G-7 consists of the leaders of: United States, Canada, Japan, Italy, United Kingdom, France and Germany.

And there appeared another wonder in heaven; and behold a great red dragon, having seven heads and ten horns, and seven crowns upon his heads (Revelation 12:3).

And I stood upon the sand of the sea, and saw a beast rise up out of the sea, having seven heads and ten horns, and upon his horns ten crowns, and upon his heads the name of blasphemy (Revelation 13:1).

Then I would know the truth of the fourth beast, which was diverse from all the others, exceeding dreadful, whose teeth were of iron, and his nails of brass; which devoured, brake in pieces, and stamped the residue with his feet;

> *And of the ten horns that were in his head, and of the*
> *other which came up, and before whom three fell; even of*
> *that horn that had eyes, and a mouth that spake very great*
> *things, whose look was more stout than his fellows* (Daniel
> 7:19).

Seven heads, ten horns and ten crowns.

The G-7 has devised a ten-region economic and global government. These ten regions will have ten leaders. Three of these economic regions will, at some point, come under the rule of one person. This one person will be the Antichrist.

The obvious omission of all Northern Europe will be the catalyst for one of the most notable fulfillments of Old Testament prophecy. The former Soviet Union has been rejected by the European Economic Community and also by the G-7. Their inability to change the opinion of their people, and their lack of productivity outside of the military establishment, has blocked their attempt at being a key player in the New World Order. This rejection, coupled with their comparative lack in basic production of goods and services, will lead to an attempt to dominate the Middle East.

The forces of the former Soviet Union with the Arab nations will attack the Middle East:

> *After many days thou shalt be visited: in the latter*
> *years thou shalt come into the land that is brought back*
> *from the sword, and is gathered out of many people, against*
> *the mountains of Israel, which have been always waste: but*
> *it is brought forth out of the nations, and they shall dwell*
> *safely all of them.*

Thou shalt ascend and come like a storm, thou shalt be like a cloud to cover the land, thou, and all thy bands, and many people with thee (Ezekial 38:8-9).

Their first target will be Egypt and the Suez Canal. Once that objective has been accomplished, they will turn their attention to Israel. In the attack on Israel, there will be a breakdown of solidarity and they will begin to fight one another.

There will also be a great earthquake. In the fighting and confusion, 5 / 6ths of all the invading armies will perish. This will take away any threat to the advancement of the global economic government—the G-7. It will also cause an outcry for someone to lead the world into peace, but what the world will get will be the worst dictator in history.

Three of the ten economic regions will consolidate into one. Three of the G-7 will be replaced by one. It could be Germany, France and Italy. They have been allied once before under a dictator. It could be that they will be once again.

There is going to be the worst war and bloodshed since the beginning of mankind.

God help us all.

In the three and one-half year reign of the Antichrist, one-half of the people of the world will perish. Water will be polluted and the atmosphere will be destroyed. One-third of all living plants will be burned up. Will all of mankind lose hope?

> *I tell you that he will avenge them speedily. Nevertheless when the Son of man cometh, shall he find faith on the earth?* (Luke 18:8).

In conjunction with all of the military warfare, there will be severe changes in the earth itself:

> *And the third angel sounded, and there fell a great star from heaven, burning as it were a lamp, and it fell upon the third part of the rivers, and upon the fountains of waters* (Revelation 8:10).

Some heavenly body will impact the earth:

> *The earth shall reel to and fro like a drunkard, and shall be removed like a cottage; and the transgression thereof shall be heavy upon it; and it shall fall, and not rise again* (Isaiah 24:20).

The changes shall be catastrophic, but those of us that shall be found in the Lord Jesus Christ will have a hope above that of the earth.

The fifth world kingdom will be the kingdom of the Lord Jesus Christ. In the reign of these kings, Jesus will return to establish His kingdom:

> *Thou sawest till that a stone was cut out without hands, which smote the image upon his feet that were of iron and clay, and brake them to pieces.*
> *Then was the iron, the clay, the brass, the silver, and the gold, broken to pieces together, and became like the chaff of the summer threshing floors; and the wind carried them*

away, that no place was found for them: and the stone that smote the image became a great mountain, and filled the whole earth (Daniel 2:34).

During the hardships ahead, the tribulation will be unprecedented for Christians as well as the unsaved. I do not write to bring despair, but to prepare. The Apostle Paul concluded that there will be some Christians alive at the return of our Lord. He states that those who are alive will be translated into spirit beings at the appearing of Christ. Therefore, we do have hope of physical survival. It will not be easy, even for those who prepare. What will happen to those following a false doctrine and a false hope?

The body of Christ—the Church—will enter into tribulation. God will have His people free of chaff and separated from the tares:

> *But ye, brethren, are not in darkness, that that day should overtake you as a thief.*
> *Ye are all the children of light, and the children of the day: we are not of the night, nor of darkness* (1 Thessalonians 5:4-5).

CHAPTER 16

WHAT TO DO

We have a hope, it's in the Lord Jesus Christ. We also have this sure word, *"We which are alive and remain unto the coming of the Lord shall not prevent them which are asleep"* (1 Thessalonians 4:15). Some of the Church who enter into the Great Tribulation will not see death until the Lord returns. Who will these be?

It will be the ones that see the events coming and prepare both mentally and physically. If we were to be thrown back into times when there weren't cars, electricity, grocery stores or machines, could we survive?

A person must examine their own situation. Do you live in a city? Do you live on a farm? Do you have any cash on hand? These are questions that may determine your chances. Cash is only good at the present time. Spend it wisely. Food, clothing and shelter are the essential things to be considered.

As quietly as possible, store these things in preparation for that day. Read the story of Joseph and the seven years of drought in the land of Egypt. This story directly relates to the Church during the Great Tribulation.

The bride of Joseph was not an Israelite, but an Egyptian. Likewise, the Bride of the Lord was not taken from among His own people. Joseph took care of his wife during the drought and the Lord will take care to provide what we need, prior to that time. We need to be observant enough to see the abundance of the Lord, able to store it up against that day.

We may well die during the tribulation, but this is the greatest of adventures that awaits the believer:

> *I knew a man in Christ above fourteen years ago, (whether in the body, I cannot tell; or whether out of the body, I cannot tell: God knoweth;) such an one caught up to the third heaven.*
>
> *And I knew such a man, (whether in the body, or out of the body, I cannot tell: God knoweth;)*
>
> *How that he was caught up into paradise, and heard unspeakable words, which it is not lawful for a man to utter* (2 Corinthians 12:2-4).

Life isn't life, death is life.

> *Verily, verily, I say unto you, Except a corn of wheat fall into the ground and die, it abideth alone: but if it die, it bringeth forth much fruit* (John 12:24).

> *For to me to live is Christ, and to die is gain* (Phillipians 1:21).

If you think in this manner, you will be ready. Are you ready?

To order additional copies of

Revealing the End of the World to the Children of Light

please send $7.99 plus &3.95 shipping & handling to:

Rev. Brent Davis
RR1 Box 495
Kiowa, OK 74553

or to order by phone,
have your credit card ready and call

1-800-917-BOOK